A Complete 2025 Travel Guide to
Kenya

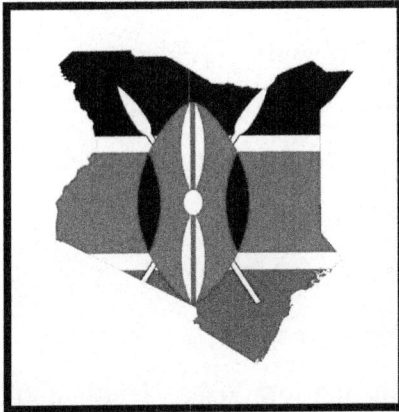

"Exploring Kenya's Majestic Wildlife, Stunning Landscapes, and Vibrant Culture"

Donald Paul S.

Sudan
Ethiopia
Uganda
Kenya
Somalia
Tanzania
Lotikipi Plain
Lake Chew Bahir
Lake Turkana
Sibiloi National Park
Malka Mari National Park
Mandera
Loima Hills
Huri Hills
Lodwar
Moyale
South Island N.P
Mt Kulal
Chalbi Desert
Bokhol Plain
South Turkana Nat. Res.
Marsabit National Reserve
Saiwa Swamp
Ndoto Hills
Losai Nat Reserve
Lake Bisina
Lake Kyoga
Kitale
Wajir
Mt. Elgon Nat. Park
Mt. Elgon
Lake Baringo
Samburu
Shaba
Kisimayo
Eldoret
Kakamega Forest
Lake Bogoria
Laikipia
Meru Nat. Park
Busia
Jinja
(Mt. Kenya Nat. Park)
Equator
Kisumu
Aberdare Nat. Park
Mt. Kenya
Lorian Swamp
Nakuru
Garissa
Lake Victoria
Ruma N.P
Lake Nakuru Nat Park
Nyeri
Embu
Lake Naivasha
Arawale Nat. Reserve
Ol Donyo Sabuk
Nairobi
Tana River Primate Nat.
Kitui
Masai Mara Game Reserve
South Kitui N.R.
Lake Magadi
Lamu
Serengeti National Park
Tsavo East
Tana River
Malindi Marine N.P.
Lake Natron
Namanga
Chyulu Hills
Amboseli
Watamu Marine Nat. Park
Ngorongoro Crater
Malindi
Watamu
Voi
Lake Manyara
Mt Kilimanjaro
Tsavo West
Arusha
Mombasa
Indian Ocean
Tarangire National Park
Lossogonoi Plateau
Shimba Hills Nat. Park
Shimoni
Pemba Island
Map not to scale:
Rough scale 1cm : 45km
see Road Travel Times
(c) www.shoortravel.com
SHOOR SAFARIS

Welcome To Kenya

Chapter 1
Introduction to Kenya

Kenya, located on the eastern coast of Africa, is a country renowned for its incredible natural beauty, rich cultural diversity, and remarkable wildlife. Known as the cradle of humanity, it boasts a wide variety of landscapes, from sun-soaked beaches along the Indian Ocean to towering mountains and expansive savannahs teeming with wildlife. Kenya is home to over 40 ethnic groups, each contributing to the nation's vibrant cultural mosaic, making it a unique and dynamic destination.

Overview of Kenya: Land of Diversity

Kenya's geographical diversity is one of its biggest draws. Visitors can explore the iconic Maasai Mara, witness the Great Migration of Wildebeest, or climb Mount Kenya, the second-highest peak in Africa. Whether you are looking for a safari adventure, a coastal retreat, or an exploration of bustling cities like Nairobi and Mombasa, Kenya has something to offer every type of traveler. Its national parks, wildlife conservancies and historical sites are globally recognized, and the country's efforts in conservation make it a model of sustainable tourism.

History and Cultural Heritage

Kenya's history is as rich as its landscapes. Archaeological evidence suggests that early human ancestors lived in the region millions of years ago. The country's modern history reflects a blend of indigenous traditions, Arab influences from the coastal trade routes, and colonial legacy from British rule. Today, Kenya's cultural diversity is manifested in its languages, art, music, and cuisine, which draw from its ethnic groups such as the Kikuyu, Maasai, Luo, and Swahili peoples. The traditions, customs, and historical stories form a significant part of the experience for travelers seeking to immerse themselves in the local culture.

Why Visit Kenya in 2025?

The year 2025 marks an exciting period for tourism in Kenya. With new developments in infrastructure, hospitality, and eco-tourism initiatives, the country is more accessible and sustainable than ever before. Special events, festivals, and conservation projects are taking place throughout the year, offering travelers a chance to engage with Kenya's natural and cultural heritage in more immersive ways. Whether you are a first-time visitor or a seasoned traveler, 2025 brings new opportunities to discover the evolving face of Kenya.

Practical Information: Visas, Health, and Safety

Traveling to Kenya is relatively straightforward, but there are important practical considerations. Most visitors will need a visa to enter Kenya, which can be obtained online through the eVisa system. Health-wise, travelers are advised to check for recommended vaccinations, including for yellow fever, typhoid, and malaria prophylaxis, depending on the region of travel. Safety is a priority, and while Kenya is generally safe for tourists, it's advisable to follow local travel advisories and be mindful of your surroundings, especially in urban centers.

Kenya's combination of natural beauty, diverse wildlife, and rich culture makes it a top destination for travelers worldwide. In 2025, it continues to offer a harmonious blend of adventure, relaxation, and learning, ensuring a memorable and transformative travel experience for all.

Chapter 2
Getting to Kenya

Kenya is a well-connected destination for international travelers, offering a variety of convenient entry points and travel options. Whether arriving by air, sea, or land, travelers can access the country through several major hubs. Understanding the best ways to get to Kenya, as well as options for transportation once inside the country, is key to planning a smooth and enjoyable trip.

International Airports and Entry Points

Kenya is serviced by several international airports, with Jomo Kenyatta International Airport (NBO) in Nairobi being the primary gateway for most visitors. This airport is one of the busiest in Africa, offering direct flights from major cities across Europe, North America, Asia, and the Middle East.

For those heading to the coast, Moi International Airport (MBA) in Mombasa is the second-largest airport and serves as a popular entry point for visitors exploring Kenya's beaches and coastal regions. Other notable airports include Kisumu International Airport (KIS), which serves the western part of the country, and Eldoret International Airport (EDL), which is often used for business and cargo flights.

In addition to air travel, Kenya has several land border crossings with neighboring countries such as Uganda, Tanzania, and Ethiopia, making it accessible by road for those traveling overland. Popular entry points include Namanga (Tanzania-Kenya border) and Busia (Uganda-Kenya border).

Flight Options and Airlines

A wide range of airlines operate flights to and from Kenya, offering flexibility in terms of price and comfort. Kenya Airways, the national carrier, operates direct flights to several global destinations, including New York, London, Paris, and Dubai. Other major international airlines serving Kenya include British Airways, Emirates, Qatar Airways, Turkish Airlines, and Ethiopian Airlines. Budget airlines such as Fly540 and Jambojet provide regional connections for travelers coming from other parts of East Africa.

For travelers looking for convenience and value, early bookings are recommended, especially during peak travel seasons such as the Great Migration (July to October) or holiday periods like Christmas and New Year. Many airlines offer seasonal promotions, so it's worth keeping an eye out for discounts on flights to Kenya.

Transportation within Kenya: Buses, Trains, and Car Rentals

Once in Kenya, getting around is relatively easy, with several transportation options available depending on your itinerary.

Buses: Inter-city buses, such as those operated by Easy Coach and Modern Coast, provide affordable transportation between major cities and towns. While bus travel is cost-effective, journeys can be long, especially on rural roads, so it's important to plan ahead for comfort.

Trains: The Standard Gauge Railway (SGR), which runs between Nairobi and Mombasa, is a popular option for travelers who want to experience the scenic landscapes of Kenya without the stress of road travel. The SGR offers both economy and first-class services, making it a comfortable and efficient way to travel between the capital and the coast.

Car Rentals: For those seeking more independence, car rentals are widely available at airports and major cities. Renting a car allows you to explore Kenya's national parks, reserves, and off-the-beaten-path destinations at your own pace. However, it's essential to familiarize yourself with Kenyan road conditions, traffic rules, and security guidelines before embarking on a self-drive adventure. Many travelers opt to hire a car with a driver, which is common in Kenya and can enhance your experience with local knowledge and navigation.

Travel Tips for First-Time Visitors

Best Time to Visit: Kenya's high tourist season is typically from June to October, coinciding with the dry season and the world-famous Great Migration in the Maasai Mara. However, other times of the year, such as the shoulder seasons (March-May and November-December), can offer lower prices and fewer crowds.

Packing Essentials: Be prepared for a wide range of climates depending on where you travel in Kenya. Nairobi and the Highlands can be cool, especially in the evenings, while the coast is typically warm and humid. Don't forget essentials like sunscreen, a hat, mosquito repellent, and comfortable shoes for safari or hiking.

Currency and Payments: The official currency is the Kenyan shilling (KES), but many hotels, safari lodges, and major retailers accept USD and credit cards. It's advisable to carry some local currency for small purchases in markets and rural areas.

Language: English and Swahili are Kenya's official languages, making it relatively easy for most travelers to communicate. However, learning a few basic Swahili phrases can enhance your interactions with locals and show respect for the culture.

Visa and Health: Ensure you have a valid visa before arriving in Kenya. The eVisa system is straightforward, allowing travelers to apply online. Additionally, make sure your vaccinations are up to date and consider travel insurance to cover any medical needs during your stay.

Getting to Kenya in 2025 is a straightforward process with a range of options for different budgets and travel styles. Whether you're flying into Nairobi for a city experience or heading straight to the coast for some relaxation, the journey to Kenya is just the beginning of your adventure in this stunning and diverse country.

Chapter 3
Top 10 Attractions in Kenya

Kenya offers a wide variety of attractions, from iconic wildlife experiences to historical and cultural landmarks. Here are the top 10 attractions, including their locations, opening hours, and the best times to visit:

Maasai Mara National Reserve

Location: Narok County, southwestern Kenya

Opening Hours: Open daily, 6:00 AM – 6:30 PM

Best Time to Visit: July to October during the Great Migration

The Maasai Mara is world-famous for its vast savannahs and abundant wildlife, especially during the annual migration of over 1.5 million wildebeest and hundreds of thousands of zebras and gazelles. It's the ultimate destination for a classic African safari.

Amboseli National Park

Location: Kajiado County, southern Kenya (near the Tanzanian border)

Opening Hours: Open daily, 6:00 AM – 6:30 PM

Best Time to Visit: June to October

Amboseli is known for its majestic views of Mount Kilimanjaro, Africa's highest peak, and large elephant herds. Visitors can see diverse wildlife and enjoy one of the best backdrops for photography in Africa.

Nairobi National Park

Location: Nairobi, just 7 km from the city center

Opening Hours: Open daily, 6:00 AM – 7:00 PM

Best Time to Visit: June to September (dry season)

Nairobi National Park offers a unique experience of a safari within a major capital city. It's home to lions, rhinos, giraffes, and over 400 species of birds. Its proximity to the city makes it an ideal day trip for travelers with limited time.

Diani Beach

Location: South Coast, Mombasa

Opening Hours: Public beach, always open

Best Time to Visit: December to March and June to September

Diani Beach is Kenya's premier beach destination, known for its pristine white sands, turquoise waters, and coral reefs. It's ideal for swimming, snorkeling, diving, and other water sports. There are also great beachfront resorts and restaurants nearby.

Lake Nakuru National Park

Location: Nakuru County, part of the Great Rift Valley

Opening Hours: Open daily, 6:00 AM – 6:30 PM

Best Time to Visit: June to March for wildlife viewing; April to June for birdwatching

Famous for its flamingos, Lake Nakuru also offers spectacular views of rhinos, lions, leopards, and other wildlife. The park is also known for its beautiful landscapes and unique acacia forests.

Lamu Old Town (Lamu Island)

Location: Lamu Island, off the northern coast of Kenya

Opening Hours: Open daily (varies by individual museums and sites)

Best Time to Visit: November to March for calm seas and warm weather

Lamu Old Town is a UNESCO World Heritage site known for its rich Swahili culture and ancient architecture. Visitors can explore narrow alleyways, historical mosques, and enjoy the relaxed pace of this traditional island town.

Mount Kenya National Park

Location: Central Kenya

Opening Hours: Open daily, 6:00 AM – 6:30 PM

Best Time to Visit: January to February and August to September (dry seasons)

Mount Kenya, Africa's second-highest mountain, offers thrilling hiking and trekking experiences. It's home to diverse flora and fauna, glaciers, and stunning alpine landscapes. The park also offers beautiful campsites for adventurous travelers.

Tsavo National Parks (East and West)

Location: Southeastern Kenya, between Nairobi and Mombasa

Opening Hours: Open daily, 6:00 AM – 6:30 PM

Best Time to Visit: May to October for the dry season

Tsavo East and West together form Kenya's largest national park. It is known for the "Red Elephants of Tsavo" and its rugged wilderness. Tsavo West offers dramatic landscapes, including Mzima Springs and the Shetani Lava Flow, while Tsavo East is more open, offering excellent wildlife viewing.

Giraffe Centre

Location: Lang'ata, Nairobi

Opening Hours: Daily, 9:00 AM – 5:00 PM

Best Time to Visit: Year-round

The Giraffe Centre is a conservation hub where visitors can learn about the endangered Rothschild giraffes and even feed them. It's a great family-friendly attraction just a short drive from Nairobi city center.

Hell's Gate National Park

Location: Naivasha, Rift Valley

Opening Hours: Open daily, 6:00 AM – 6:30 PM

Best Time to Visit: June to March

Hell's Gate is known for its striking landscapes, including cliffs, gorges, and geothermal springs. Visitors can hike, rock climb, or cycle through the park, making it one of Kenya's most unique and adventurous destinations.

These top 10 attractions showcase Kenya's diverse offerings, from wildlife-rich national parks to stunning coastal and cultural sites. Each location offers something different, and planning your visit around the best times will ensure you have the most memorable experience possible.

Chapter 4
Safari Planning Guide

A safari in Kenya is a once-in-a-lifetime adventure, offering the chance to witness some of the world's most incredible wildlife up close in their natural habitats. From the iconic Big Five (lion, leopard, elephant, buffalo, and rhino) to breathtaking landscapes, a well-planned safari is essential to make the most of your experience. This guide will help you navigate the key elements of planning a safari in Kenya, including selecting the best parks, choosing the right safari package, and tips for sustainable and ethical travel.

Best National Parks and Reserves for Safari

Kenya has over 50 national parks and reserves, each offering unique wildlife experiences and scenery. Here are some of the top destinations:

Maasai Mara National Reserve

Famous for the Great Migration and Big Five sightings, the Maasai Mara is Kenya's most iconic safari destination. It's especially popular for wildlife photography and balloon safaris.

Best Time to Visit: July to October (for the Great Migration)

Amboseli National Park

Known for large elephant herds and its views of Mount Kilimanjaro, Amboseli offers excellent year-round game viewing and is a top choice for elephant lovers.

Best Time to Visit: June to October (dry season)

Tsavo East & Tsavo West National Parks

Together, these parks form Kenya's largest protected area. Tsavo East is famous for its "Red Elephants," while Tsavo West offers volcanic landscapes and the stunning Mzima Springs.

Best Time to Visit: May to October (dry season)

Lake Nakuru National Park

Known for its flamingo-covered shores and rhino sanctuary, Lake Nakuru is perfect for birdwatchers and wildlife enthusiasts alike.

Best Time to Visit: June to March

Samburu National Reserve

A lesser-known gem, Samburu is home to unique species such as the Grevy's zebra, the reticulated giraffe, and the Somali ostrich. Its semi-arid landscape offers a different safari experience from the savannahs.

Best Time to Visit: June to October (dry season)

Laikipia Plateau

This region is known for its private conservancies and offers more exclusive and sustainable safari experiences. It's ideal for those seeking privacy and luxury.

Best Time to Visit: June to October

Choosing a Safari Package: Budget, Mid-Range, Luxury

Safari packages in Kenya come in various price ranges, from budget-friendly tours to ultra-luxurious experiences. Here's a breakdown of what to expect from each category:

Budget Safari

Typical Cost: $100 to $200 per day

Accommodation: Basic campsites, tented camps, or budget lodges

Transport: Shared safari vehicles (usually minivans or 4x4s)

Inclusions: Game drives, meals, park fees

Ideal For: Backpackers, solo travelers, and those looking for a more affordable safari experience

Mid-Range Safari

Typical Cost: $250 to $400 per day
Accommodation: Comfortable lodges, tented camps with en-suite facilities

Transport: Private or shared 4x4 safari vehicles

Inclusions: Game drives, meals, park fees, sometimes additional activities like guided walks or cultural visits

Ideal For: Couples, families, and small groups looking for a balance of comfort and adventure

Luxury Safari

Typical Cost: $500 to $1,500+ per day

Accommodation: Luxury lodges, tented camps, private reserves, exclusive-use properties

Transport: Private 4x4s, air transfers, or charter flights

Inclusions: All-inclusive meals, drinks, premium service, private game drives, often with expert guides and personalized itineraries

Ideal For: Honeymooners, high-end travelers, and those seeking exclusive, personalized safari experiences

Wildlife Encounters: The Big Five and Beyond

Kenya is famous for the Big Five, but it offers much more than that. Here are some of the key species and experiences to look out for:

Big Five: Lion, leopard, elephant, buffalo, and rhino. These can be spotted in the Maasai Mara, Amboseli, Tsavo, and other top reserves.

Unique Species: Samburu is known for rare species such as the Grevy's zebra, reticulated giraffe, and gerenuk.

Birdwatching: Lake Nakuru and the Rift Valley lakes are excellent for birdwatching, especially flamingos and pelicans.

Great Migration: From July to October, witness the awe-inspiring migration of wildebeest and zebras in the Maasai Mara.

Sustainable and Ethical Travel Tips

Sustainability is increasingly important when planning a safari, as Kenya's wildlife and natural habitats need protection for future generations. Here are some tips for responsible safari travel:

Choose Eco-Friendly Lodges

Many safari camps and lodges in Kenya operate on sustainable principles, from reducing plastic use to supporting local communities. Look for eco-certified accommodations that have initiatives in conservation and sustainability.

Support Local Communities

Consider booking with companies that involve local communities in their operations, providing jobs, and promoting education. Some safari lodges have programs where a portion of your stay helps fund local projects like schools or wildlife conservation.

Minimize Environmental Impact

Stick to designated safari trails to avoid damaging ecosystems, and follow your guide's instructions closely. Carry reusable water bottles and avoid single-use plastics wherever possible.

Wildlife Ethics

Never disturb or feed wildlife. Keep a safe distance from animals, and always respect their natural behaviors. Avoid attractions that exploit animals, such as unethical elephant riding or close encounters with captive wildlife.

Leave No Trace

Be mindful of litter and waste. Take all the rubbish with you and dispose of it responsibly. Help preserve the pristine beauty of Kenya's natural landscapes.

Best Time to Visit for a Safari

The best time for a safari in Kenya largely depends on what you want to see and your weather preferences. Here's a general guide:

Dry Season (June to October): This is the prime time for safaris, as the weather is dry and animals are easier to spot around water sources. This period also coincides with the Great Migration in the Maasai Mara.

Short Rains (November to December): Although wildlife viewing is still good, the rains can make it slightly harder to spot animals. However, this is also a less crowded and more affordable time to visit.

Long Rains (March to May): This is the low season for safaris, as heavy rains make roads muddy and some lodges may close. However, it's an excellent time for birdwatching and seeing lush green landscapes.

By carefully planning your safari based on your interests, budget, and preferred travel style, you can ensure that your Kenyan safari experience will be unforgettable. From iconic wildlife sightings to immersive cultural encounters, Kenya offers a rich array of safari options for every traveler.

Chapter 5
Kenyan Culture and Traditions

Kenya's culture and traditions are as diverse as its people, with each ethnic group contributing unique customs, music, art, and beliefs to the nation's identity. From vibrant music and dance forms to meaningful rituals and traditional ceremonies, Kenyan culture is deeply rooted in its history and values. Many Kenyan traditions continue to thrive today, serving as a bridge between past and present and offering travelers a chance to experience the authenticity of Kenyan life.

Family and Community Structure

Family and community lie at the heart of Kenyan culture. Most communities are organized into extended family networks, which provide support and foster unity among members. Respect for elders and kinship ties are emphasized across all ethnic groups, with family gatherings and community events are common ways to celebrate milestones and maintain connections.

Marriage and Courtship

Marriage is a highly valued institution in Kenya, with traditional wedding ceremonies featuring elaborate rituals, music, and dances. The process of courtship and marriage varies among tribes, often involving dowries, negotiations between families, and community blessings. In Kikuyu culture, for instance, there is a ceremonial "ruracio" (bride price negotiation), while Maasai and Samburu traditions incorporate unique attire and blessings from elders.

Gender Roles

Traditional gender roles are still present in rural areas, where men and women have distinct responsibilities. However, gender roles are evolving, especially in urban centers, where more women are pursuing education, careers, and political roles.

Traditional Clothing

Kenyan traditional attire is colorful, symbolic, and varies widely between tribes.

Maasai Shukas: The Maasai wear brightly colored cloths called "shukas," often in red or blue patterns, along with elaborate beaded jewelry.

Kikuyu: The Kikuyu people wear black, brown, and white robes or wraps, particularly during cultural events. Kikuyu women also wear colorful beaded necklaces.

Swahili Kanga and Kitenge: Along the coast, Swahili women wear brightly colored "kangas" (cloths with Swahili sayings) and "kitenge" fabrics, while men may wear "kofia" caps and light robes.

Turkana and Samburu Adornments: Turkana and Samburu tribes are known for their intricate beadwork, jewelry, and elaborate headdresses.

Traditional dress is often reserved for special occasions, while many Kenyans wear Western-style clothing in daily life.

Kenyan Music and Dance

Music and dance are essential elements of Kenyan culture, playing roles in celebrations, storytelling, and rites of passage. Each tribe has unique styles, instruments, and rhythms.

Benga Music: A popular genre originating with the Luo community, Benga is lively, guitar-driven music that is widely appreciated across Kenya.

Taarab: Originating from the coastal Swahili culture, Taarab blends Arabic, Indian, and African influences using instruments like the oud and percussion.

Isukuti Dance: A traditional Luhya dance performed during celebrations, known for its powerful drumming and energetic moves.

Maasai Adumu Dance: Known as the "jumping dance," this ritual features Maasai men performing impressive vertical jumps to demonstrate strength and endurance.

Ohangla: Popular among the Luo, Ohangla music features fast-paced drumming and is often played during weddings and celebrations.

Kenyan artists are also incorporating modern styles like hip-hop, reggae, and Afropop into their music, creating a dynamic and evolving music scene.

Cuisine and Dining Traditions

Kenyan cuisine is a delicious fusion of local ingredients, spices, and culinary influences from India, the Middle East, and Europe. Here are some traditional dishes you're likely to encounter:

Ugali: A staple across Kenya, ugali is a maize-based porridge or dough that's often served with vegetables, meat, or stew.

Nyama Choma: This popular dish of grilled meat (often goat or beef) is enjoyed at gatherings, accompanied by kachumbari (a tomato and onion salad).

Sukuma Wiki: A simple dish of collard greens sautéed with onions and tomatoes, typically served alongside ugali.

Pilau and Biryani: Influenced by Swahili culture along the coast, these spiced rice dishes include meat or fish and are commonly enjoyed at special occasions.

Chapati: A flatbread borrowed from Indian cuisine, chapati is often paired with stews or vegetables.

Dining Etiquette

In Kenya, sharing food is a common way to show hospitality. When dining with locals, it's polite to wash hands before meals (often provided for by a communal bowl in rural areas) and to wait for elders or hosts to start eating first.

Traditional Beliefs and Spirituality

Many Kenyans observe traditional beliefs alongside Christianity and Islam, which are the predominant religions. Traditional spirituality often involves reverence for ancestors, nature, and spiritual leaders within the community. Rites of passage, such as initiations, births, and marriages, are sacred ceremonies conducted with blessings from elders and sometimes include sacrifices or prayers to ancestors.

Rituals and Rites of Passage

Circumcision Ceremonies: For many tribes, including the Kikuyu, Kalenjin, and Maasai, circumcision is an important rite of passage marking the transition to adulthood.

Elders and Blessings: Elders hold a respected place in society, offering blessings during life events and acting as custodians of traditions and knowledge.

Art and Craftsmanship

Kenya is known for its diverse artistry and craftsmanship, with traditional art forms that include:

Beadwork: Maasai, Turkana, and Samburu tribes create intricate beadwork that symbolizes social status, age, and clan affiliations.

Wood Carving: Akamba artisans are renowned for their wooden carvings, particularly animal sculptures, masks, and decorative items, often available at markets.

Pottery and Baskets: Luhya and Kamba women are skilled in weaving baskets and making pottery, which are used in daily life as well as for sale in local markets.

Soapstone Carvings: Found mainly in Kisii, soapstone carvings are a popular Kenyan craft and range from abstract art to animal figurines.

Artisans continue to use these skills to create contemporary art, merging traditional styles with modern influences.

Festivals and Celebrations

Kenya's festivals highlight its rich cultural diversity, allowing visitors to experience the vibrancy of Kenyan traditions.

Mombasa Carnival: Celebrated on Kenya's coast, this festival showcases Swahili culture with parades, traditional dances, and musical performances.

Lamu Cultural Festival: A celebration of the island's heritage, with dhow races, donkey races, and Swahili poetry and cuisine.

Maasai Mara Cultural Festival: A gathering to honor Maasai traditions, featuring dancing, warrior competitions, and cultural displays.

Kenya Music Festival: A national event that brings together performers from schools and communities across the country, celebrating traditional music, dance, and drama.

International Camel Derby: Held annually in Maralal, this unique event combines camel racing with cultural festivities, attracting visitors and participants from all over Kenya.

Cultural Etiquette and Respect for Traditions

When visiting Kenya, it's important to show respect for local customs and traditions.

Greetings: Kenyans value greetings, and it's polite to greet others with a handshake or traditional greeting. In some cultures, like the Maasai, spitting lightly on the hand is a sign of respect.

Respecting Elders: Elders are respected across Kenya, and visitors are encouraged to show deference when interacting with them.

Modesty in Dress: Especially in rural or conservative areas, dress modestly to respect local norms, particularly when visiting religious sites.

Photography: Always ask permission before photographing people or cultural sites, as some communities are sensitive about photography.

Kenya's culture is an intricate tapestry of tradition, spirituality, and community values, offering travelers a window into the lives of its diverse people. Experiencing Kenya's culture firsthand allows visitors to connect more deeply with the spirit of the nation, creating memories that last well beyond the trip itself.

Chapter 6
Accomdation In Kenya

Kenya's major cities, particularly Nairobi, Mombasa, and Kisumu, offer a broad range of hotels and lodges catering to luxury, comfort, and unique experiences.

Nairobi

Giraffe Manor is a standout boutique hotel, offering an exceptional experience where guests can interact with resident giraffes. It's a perfect choice for those looking for luxury with a touch of wildlife

The Sarova Panafric Hotel provides a blend of elegance and comfort, offering stunning views of Nairobi's skyline. It's a favorite for both business and leisure travelers

The Fairview Hotel, known for its lush gardens and central location, offers a quieter alternative for travelers who prefer a more relaxed setting in the city center

Mombasa

The Sarova Whitesands Beach Resort & Spa is one of the most famous beach resorts, offering luxurious accommodations with direct access to Mombasa's pristine beaches

Voyager Beach Resort is another excellent option for families and groups, with its all-inclusive package and beachside activities

The Reef Hotel offers affordable and comfortable stays near Mombasa's main attractions, making it an ideal choice for those seeking a more budget-friendly option near the coast

Kisumu

The Vic Hotel Kisumu is a top choice in Kisumu, providing modern amenities and views of Lake Victoria. It's a favorite for business travelers and tourists alike

Dunga Hill Camp offers a more rustic but scenic lakeside experience with eco-lodges, perfect for those looking to enjoy nature in a tranquil environment

These hotels and lodges represent just a few of the best accommodations available in Kenya's key cities, offering diverse options for every type of traveler. Whether you're seeking luxury or a more rustic adventure, there's something for everyone.

Safari Lodges: Unique Experiences in the Wild

Kenya's safari lodges offer unforgettable experiences, combining luxury and wilderness in renowned national parks and reserves like the Maasai Mara, Amboseli, and Samburu. These lodges emphasize comfort, immersion in nature, and unique encounters with wildlife, making each stay memorable.

Mahali Mzuri, Maasai Mara

Owned by Sir Richard Branson, Mahali Mzuri is an eco-conscious luxury camp set in the private Olare Motorogi Conservancy. Known for its breathtaking views, exclusive game drives, and commitment to sustainable tourism, Mahali Mzuri provides guests with close-up encounters with the "Big Five" and a chance to experience the Great Migration from June to October. The camp features luxury tents with private decks and infinity pools overlooking the Mara's sweeping plains

Loisaba Tented Camp—Laikipia

Loisaba offers a luxurious yet eco-friendly experience in northern Kenya's Laikipia region, famous for its stunning landscapes and elephant populations. Known for its "Star Beds," where guests sleep under the open sky on rolling platforms, the camp provides a truly unique safari experience. Visitors can enjoy game drives, guided nature walks, and even camel safaris in this conservancy, which supports local communities and wildlife conservation

Ol Donyo Lodge, Chyulu Hills

Nestled between Amboseli and Tsavo, Ol Donyo Lodge boasts spectacular views of Mount Kilimanjaro and offers intimate wildlife encounters in a secluded setting. The lodge's suites have rooftop terraces with "star beds" for open-air sleeping and private pools, perfect for a romantic getaway. Activities include horseback safaris, mountain biking, and guided walks. Ol Donyo is part of the Great Plains Conservation initiative, emphasizing conservation and community empowerment

Saruni Samburu— Samburu National Reserve

This lodge is known for its panoramic views over Kalama Conservancy and the Northern Frontier District. Saruni Samburu offers an immersive cultural experience where guests can engage with Samburu guides and learn about local traditions. The lodge's minimalist, open-plan villas overlook dramatic landscapes, providing a perfect mix of luxury and raw nature. Safari activities include night drives and visits to a nearby elephant sanctuary

Angama Mara-Maasai Mara

Situated on the edge of the Great Rift Valley, Angama Mara offers sweeping views of the Maasai Mara and was even the filming site for Out of Africa. With floor-to-ceiling windows in each suite, guests can enjoy unparalleled views of the Mara from the comfort of their rooms. The lodge specializes in hot-air balloon safaris, which offer a bird's-eye view of wildlife and landscapes at sunrise. Guided walking tours and cultural visits to Maasai villages are also popular activities

These safari lodges offer travelers a perfect blend of adventure, luxury, and responsible tourism. With exclusive experiences like star beds, hot-air balloon safaris, and cultural interactions, each stay promises an exceptional, immersive connection with Kenya's wild landscapes.

Budget Stays and Backpacker Options

For travelers exploring Kenya on a budget, there are plenty of affordable stays and backpacker-friendly options. From budget-friendly hostels and guesthouses in Nairobi to affordable safari camps, these accommodations cater to those looking to experience Kenya's beauty and culture without overspending.

Kenya Youth Hostels: Nairobi, Mombasa, and Kisumu

Kenya's youth hostels provide affordable, comfortable lodging options across the country. In Nairobi, the Kenya Youth Hostel Association (KYHA), offers a secure, budget-friendly stay with shared rooms, communal kitchens, and tour services. In Mombasa, there are similar hostels close to the beach, making them ideal for budget travelers looking to explore the coastal region

Wildebeest Eco Camp, Nairobi

Wildebeest Eco Camp provides a budget-friendly safari experience close to Nairobi National Park. The camp offers dormitories, safari tents, and small private rooms, making it a popular choice among backpackers. With an emphasis on eco-friendly practices, guests can enjoy the natural setting while taking advantage of affordable day trips to Nairobi's main attractions

Distant Relatives Eco-Lodge & Backpackers – Kilifi

Located along the Kenyan coast in Kilifi, Distant Relatives is a unique eco-lodge and hostel combining budget accommodations with a vibrant social atmosphere. Backpackers can choose from dorms, private rooms, and camping. The lodge organizes activities like snorkeling, beach clean-ups, and community projects, making it a great choice for eco-conscious travelers who want to interact with locals and explore Kenya's beautiful coastline

Camp Carnelley's—Lake Naivasha

Camp Carnelley's near Lake Naivasha offers rustic, affordable lodging perfect for backpackers and budget travelers. With options ranging from dorms to private cabins, this campsite has a relaxed atmosphere with easy access to Lake Naivasha's outdoor activities like hiking, boat rides, and visits to Hell's Gate National Park. The camp's restaurant and bar add a social vibe, making it a favorite among budget travelers

Sentrim Tsavo East Camp—Tsavo East National Park

For budget safari options, Sentrim Tsavo East Camp provides a more affordable way to experience a safari in Tsavo East National Park. This camp offers basic but comfortable tented accommodations and standard rooms, allowing guests to enjoy wildlife safaris at a fraction of the cost of luxury camps. Sentrim's organized safari tours make it easy for budget travelers to enjoy Kenya's wildlife

These budget stays provide economical options for travelers seeking adventure and cultural immersion in Kenya without the high cost. Whether staying in the city, on the coast, or near the national parks, budget travelers can still enjoy memorable, authentic experiences in Kenya.

Eco-Lodges and Sustainable Tourism
Kenya's eco-lodges offer travelers sustainable ways to explore the country's stunning landscapes and wildlife while minimizing environmental impact and supporting local communities. Located in remote national parks and lesser-explored areas, these lodges promote eco-friendly practices and provide a unique, immersive experience that aligns with responsible tourism principles.

Ol Pejeta Bush Camp, Laikipia
Ol Pejeta Bush Camp, located in the Ol Pejeta Conservancy in Laikipia, is a prime example of sustainable tourism. This tented camp operates with a low environmental footprint and supports

local wildlife conservation efforts, including the protection of endangered species like the northern white rhino. Guests can participate in conservation-focused activities such as tracking rhinos and learning about anti-poaching efforts while staying in eco-conscious accommodations powered by solar energy

Campi ya Kanzi—Chyulu Hills

Campi ya Kanzi, nestled in the Chyulu Hills, is a luxury eco-lodge partnered with the local Maasai community to promote conservation and economic empowerment. It operates on sustainable practices, using solar energy and rainwater collection, and has minimal impact on the land. By staying at Campi ya Kanzi, guests directly contribute to the Maasai Wilderness Conservation Trust, which funds health, education, and environmental programs for the Maasai community

Eagle View—Mara Naboisho Conservancy

Located in the Mara Naboisho Conservancy near the Maasai Mara, Eagle View Lodge offers eco-friendly accommodations that blend into the surrounding savanna. The lodge works closely with the local Maasai community, providing jobs and sharing revenue to support the community and conservation efforts. Eagle View emphasizes sustainable tourism through solar-powered energy, water conservation, and waste reduction, allowing guests to enjoy safaris with minimal impact on the environment

Borana Lodge, Laikipia

Borana Lodge is part of the Borana Conservancy, a sanctuary for endangered species in Laikipia. The lodge operates on 100% renewable energy and prioritizes wildlife conservation by reinvesting tourism revenue into anti-poaching efforts and land restoration. It is home to rhinos, elephants, and lions, and guests can participate in conservation activities like ranger-led patrols and rhino monitoring, offering a deep understanding of Kenya's conservation landscape

Distant Relatives Eco-Lodge & Backpackers – Kilifi

On Kenya's coast, Distant Relatives Eco-Lodge & Backpackers offers an affordable eco-friendly stay with a focus on community and environmental sustainability. The lodge uses compost toilets, solar energy, and rainwater harvesting, creating a low-impact accommodation option. Located near Kilifi Creek, it encourages eco-conscious travel with activities like beach clean-ups and community engagement programs, making it popular with backpackers interested in sustainable tourism

Kenya's eco-lodges exemplify sustainable tourism through conservation, community engagement, and eco-conscious operations. These lodges allow travelers to connect with Kenya's natural beauty and wildlife responsibly, supporting efforts to preserve the country's landscapes and benefit local communities.

Chapter 7
Adventure and Outdoor
Activities

Kenya is a premier destination for adventure and outdoor enthusiasts, offering diverse landscapes that range from mountains and savannas to coastlines and lakes. Whether you're looking to hike rugged terrain, dive into coral reefs, or explore the savanna on a safari, Kenya's natural beauty and array of activities provide something for every traveler.

Hiking and Mountain Climbing

Kenya's mountains and scenic landscapes provide a variety of hiking options for all levels of experience.

Mount Kenya

Location: Central Kenya, Mount Kenya National Park

Highlights: Kenya's highest mountain, Mount Kenya (5,199 meters), is a UNESCO World Heritage Site. Site and offers challenging climbing routes up

Batian and Nelion peaks, as well as more accessible treks like Point Lenana. Hikers pass through bamboo forests, moorlands, and unique Afro-alpine landscapes.

Best Time to Visit: January to March and June to October for clear skies and favorable climbing conditions.

Aberdare Ranges
Location: Aberdare National Park, Central Kenya
Highlights: This range offers shorter day hikes and multi-day trekking options with stunning views of valleys, waterfalls, and wildlife. Notable hikes include Karuru Falls and Elephant Hill.

Best Time to Visit: June to October for cooler, drier conditions.

Wildlife Safaris and Game Drives

Kenya's safari experience is world-renowned, with a variety of ecosystems and abundant wildlife.

Maasai Mara National Reserve

Highlights: Known for the annual Great Migration, the Mara offers sightings of lions, elephants, rhinos, and more. Safari options range from budget camping safaris to luxury lodges.

Best Time to Visit: July to October for the migration, though wildlife viewing is good year-round.

Amboseli National Park

Highlights: Amboseli is famous for its stunning views of Mount Kilimanjaro and large elephant herds. The park's landscape is diverse, with swamps, savannas, and open plains.

Best Time to Visit: June to October and January to February, when wildlife is easiest to spot.

Beach and Water Sports

Kenya's coastlines along the Indian Ocean are ideal for beach vacations and water sports.

Diani Beach

Activities: Diani Beach, with its white sand and turquoise waters, is perfect for swimming snorkeling, kite surfing, and jet skiing. The area also has coral reefs for diving enthusiasts.

Best Time to Visit: December to April for warm waters and clear visibility.

Malindi and Watamu Marine National Park

Activities: These parks offer snorkeling and diving among coral reefs, home to diverse marine life like sea turtles, dolphins, and tropical fish. Boat tours and dolphin watching are popular.

Best Time to Visit: November to April for optimal underwater visibility.

Hot Air Ballooning

One of the most unique ways to experience Kenya's landscapes is through a hot air balloon ride.

Maasai Mara Balloon Safari

Highlights: Soaring over the Maasai Mara at sunrise offers breathtaking views of the savanna, rivers, and wildlife from above. Many rides end with a champagne breakfast in the bush.

Best Time to Visit: July to October during the Great Migration for incredible animal sightings.

Bird Watching

Kenya is a paradise for bird watchers, with over 1,100 species recorded.

Lake Nakuru National Park

Highlights: Known for its flocks of pink flamingos, Lake Nakuru also hosts pelicans, eagles, and over 400 bird species.

Best Time to Visit: Year-round, though April to June is ideal for birding.

Lake Naivasha

Highlights: This freshwater lake is home to a variety of water birds, including cormorants, herons, and African fish eagles.

Best Time to Visit: November to April, when migratory birds are present.

Whitewater Rafting and Kayaking

For those looking for a rush, Kenya's rivers offer exciting rafting and kayaking experiences.

Tana River

Highlights: Located near Sagana, the Tana River offers thrilling rapids (class II-IV) suitable for both beginners and seasoned rafters. Kayaking is also popular here.

Best Time to Visit: April to May for the most intense rapids, though the river is accessible year-round.

Cycling and Mountain Biking

Kenya's varied terrain makes it ideal for cycling and mountain biking, with routes available for different skill levels.

Hell's Gate National Park

Highlights: One of the few parks in Kenya where visitors can cycle among wildlife, Hell's Gate offers scenic bike trails through gorges and past geothermal features, and alongside zebras, gazelles, and giraffes.

Best Time to Visit: Year-round, though mornings and evenings are cooler.

Ngong Hills

Highlights: These iconic hills near Nairobi offer challenging climbs and rewarding views. Cyclists can navigate trails through eucalyptus forests and rolling hills.

Best Time to Visit: June to October for dry, cooler weather.

Caving and Rock Climbing

Kenya's rock formations and caves provide plenty of options for climbers and spelunkers.

Fischers Tower and Central Tower at Hell's Gate

Highlights: Popular for rock climbing, with routes suitable for beginners and advanced climbers. Climbs offer spectacular views of the park and its wildlife.

Best Time to Visit: July to September, when temperatures are cooler.

Kenya's Lava Caves

Highlights: Located near Mount Suswa, these caves are ideal for adventurous cavers. The network of lava tunnels and caverns is a unique experience, often guided by local experts.

Best Time to Visit: June to October for easier access.

Camel Safaris

For a unique experience, camel safaris provide a leisurely way to explore Kenya's arid regions.

Laikipia and Samburu Regions

Highlights: Camel safaris in these semi-arid landscapes offer visitors a chance to explore remote areas, guided by Samburu or Maasai locals. Multi-day tours are available, with overnight stays in camps under the stars.

Best Time to Visit: June to October, and January to February for cooler weather.

Cultural Tours and Village Visits

Kenya's adventure offerings aren't limited to nature; cultural immersion can be just as enriching.

Maasai Village Tours

Highlights: Visiting a traditional Maasai village provides insight into local customs, traditional crafts, and daily life. Guests may witness traditional dances, craft-making, and meet elders.

Best Time to Visit: Year-round.

Turkana Festival

Highlights: Held annually in the Turkana region, this festival showcases the traditions, music, and dances of Kenya's diverse northern communities. It's an exciting way to learn about the country's ethnic diversity.

Best Time to Visit: May each year.

Kenya's outdoor adventures and cultural experiences make it an unparalleled destination for those looking to explore, learn, and connect with nature and people. Whether it's a safari on the savanna, climbing high-altitude peaks, or learning ancient traditions, Kenya offers endless ways to make unforgettable memories.

Chapter 8
Kenya's Natural Wonders

Kenya is celebrated for its stunning natural landscapes, from iconic mountains and expansive savannas to serene lakes and lush forests. Each of these natural wonders offers breathtaking beauty and opportunities for exploration, providing visitors with unforgettable views, wildlife sightings, and a deep sense of connection to Kenya's diverse ecosystems. Here are some of the most remarkable natural wonders to experience on your journey through Kenya.

The Great Rift Valley

The Great Rift Valley, a geological marvel stretching approximately 6,000 kilometers from Lebanon to Mozambique, bisects Kenya and creates some of the country's most iconic landscapes. Formed by tectonic shifts millions of years ago, the Rift Valley is a striking expanse of escarpments, lakes, mountains, and plains, all rich with biodiversity and stunning views. It serves as a natural haven for wildlife, a geological wonder, and a cultural heartland for various communities.

Formation and Geology of the Great Rift Valley

Description: The Great Rift Valley was formed by the Earth's tectonic plates pulling apart, creating a series of fractures and depressions. This geological activity led to the formation of many deep lakes, fertile valleys, and volcanic formations that make up the valley's unique landscape. Along Kenya's stretch of the Rift Valley, visitors encounter high escarpments, geothermal springs, and a series of lakes that support diverse ecosystems.

Geological Highlights: Some of the Valley's most dramatic features include the cliffs of the Mau Escarpment, geothermal activity around Lake Bogoria, and volcanic formations like Mount Longonot and Suswa.

The Rift Valley Lakes

The Rift Valley is home to several remarkable lakes, each with its own ecosystem and scenic beauty:

Lake Nakuru

Highlights: Known for the famous flocks of pink flamingos that gather here, Lake Nakuru is a saline lake in Lake Nakuru National Park. It's home to various wildlife, including black and white rhinos, and is a birdwatcher's paradise with over 400 bird species.

Best Time to Visit: July to December for birding; wildlife can be seen year-round.

Lake Naivasha

Highlights: Lake Naivasha, a freshwater lake, offers boat rides, birdwatching, and hippo sightings. Nearby, Crescent Island Sanctuary allows visitors to walk among giraffes, zebras, and antelope. The lake is an oasis with a rich ecosystem supporting many species of birds and mammals.

Best Time to Visit: Year-round, though dry months are ideal for walking safaris.

Lake Bogoria

Highlights: This soda lake is famous for its hot springs and geysers, along with large flamingo flocks. The geothermal activity at Lake Bogoria offers a unique landscape, with steaming geysers adding to its surreal, otherworldly beauty.

Best Time to Visit: November to April for birdwatching.

Lake Turkana

Highlights: Known as the "Jade Sea" due to its color, Lake Turkana is the world's largest desert lake and holds significant archaeological sites with ancient hominid fossils. The lake's remote, rugged beauty and abundant fish populations make it one of Kenya's most unique destinations.

Best Time to Visit: December to March, when temperatures are moderate.

Mount Longonot and Suswa

Mount Longonot

Location: Near Lake Naivasha

Highlights: An extinct stratovolcano, Mount Longonot is a popular hiking destination offering views into a crater covered with forest. A trek to the summit provides a panoramic view of the Rift Valley and surrounding landscapes.

Best Time to Visit: June to October and January to February for cooler, dry weather.

Mount Suswa

Location: Southeast of Lake Naivasha

Highlights: Mount Suswa features a double crater and a series of caves, with a diverse wildlife population that includes baboons, leopards, and hyenas. The lava tube caves around the mountain are particularly popular among adventurous visitors.

Best Time to Visit: June to October.

Hell's Gate National Park

Location: Near Lake Naivasha

Highlights: Hell's Gate offers stunning cliffs, gorges, and geothermal activity, and is one of Kenya's few parks where visitors can walk or cycle among wildlife. Visitors can explore towering cliffs, hot springs, and wildlife such as zebras, buffaloes, and gazelles.

Best Time to Visit: Year-round, with June to October offering cooler, dry weather.

Hell's Gate inspired the scenery in Disney's The Lion King and is also home to the Olkaria Geothermal Spa, where visitors can enjoy hot springs within the park.

Aberdare Ranges and Escarpments

Location: Central Rift Valley

Highlights: The Aberdare Ranges offer stunning mountainous landscapes and waterfalls, including the impressive Karuru Falls. It's also home to dense forests with rare wildlife such as the elusive bongo antelope, making it a top destination for both hiking and wildlife watching.

Best Time to Visit: June to October for clear hiking paths.

The Aberdare region is a lush contrast to the drier regions of the Rift Valley, and the scenic escarpments offer stunning viewpoints over the valley below.

Cultural Significance

The Rift Valley is home to various ethnic groups and has a rich cultural heritage, especially among the Maasai, Samburu, Turkana, and Kikuyu communities. Many areas in the Rift Valley are dotted with traditional villages where visitors can engage with local communities and learn about their customs, crafts, and way of life.

Key Experiences: Visiting Maasai villages, attending local festivals, and experiencing traditional dances, handicrafts, and ceremonies.

The Great Rift Valley is an extraordinary natural and cultural destination, providing visitors with opportunities for wildlife encounters, scenic landscapes, outdoor activities, and cultural immersion. With its blend of breathtaking topography, unique lakes, volcanic mountains, and vibrant communities, the Rift Valley remains a must-see highlight in Kenya.

Lakes and Waterfalls

Kenya is graced with a number of beautiful lakes and waterfalls that add to its rich and diverse natural landscape. Each water body, whether lake or waterfall, contributes to the country's biodiversity and offers opportunities for adventure, relaxation, and sightseeing. From the pink-dotted shores of Lake Nakuru to the powerful plunge of Karuru Falls, Kenya's lakes and waterfalls showcase nature at its finest. Here's a guide to exploring some of the country's most remarkable water features.

Lake Nakuru

Location: Rift Valley, Lake Nakuru National Park

Highlights: Famous for its vibrant pink flamingo flocks, Lake Nakuru is a shallow soda lake with alkaline waters that attract an array of bird species, including pelicans and cormorants. The lake is also home to a large population of white and black rhinos, zebras, and giraffes.

Best Time to Visit: July to December for optimal birdwatching, although wildlife viewing is excellent year-round.

The backdrop of the Mau Escarpment and the surrounding savannah add to Lake Nakuru's appeal, making it an ideal spot for nature lovers and photographers.

Lake Naivasha

Location: Near Naivasha Town, Rift Valley Province

Highlights: A freshwater lake and a peaceful retreat, Lake Naivasha is popular for boat rides and birdwatching, offering sightings of hippos, fish eagles, and kingfishers. Nearby, the Crescent Island Sanctuary provides a unique opportunity to walk among giraffes, zebras, and antelopes.

Best Time to Visit: Year-round, though dry seasons (January to March, July to October) are ideal for clear skies and safaris.

Lake Naivasha's serene waters and abundant flora and fauna make it a relaxing stopover, especially after a safari.

Lake Bogoria

Location: Rift Valley Province

Highlights: Known for its geothermal hot springs and geysers, Lake Bogoria is a saline, alkaline lake that draws flamingos and other bird species. The high saline levels produce vibrant algae blooms, attracting hundreds of thousands of flamingos, which create a surreal pink landscape.

Best Time to Visit: November to April for birdwatching and geyser activity.

Visitors can experience the heat of the springs and marvel at the boiling geysers along the lake's shoreline, but swimming is not advised due to the high temperatures.

Lake Turkana
Location: Northern Kenya, bordering Ethiopia
Highlights: Known as the "Jade Sea" due to its mesmerizing green-blue color, Lake Turkana is the world's largest desert lake and a UNESCO World Heritage Site. Its remote beauty, unique volcanic islands, and rich archaeological sites (including some of the oldest hominid fossils) make it a truly extraordinary destination.

Best Time to Visit: December to March and July to October for milder temperatures.

Lake Turkana's stark, otherworldly landscape, combined with its cultural and historical significance, attracts adventurous travelers and researchers alike.

Lake Victoria

Location: Bordering Kenya, Uganda, and Tanzania

Highlights: As Africa's largest freshwater lake, Lake Victoria supports a vast ecosystem and provides sustenance for numerous communities around it. Activities include fishing, birdwatching, and exploring the lake's islands, such as Rusinga and Mfangano.

Best Time to Visit: Year-round, though the dry season is ideal for water activities.

Fishing villages along Lake Victoria offer insights into local culture and the lake's role in the local economy.

Karuru Falls

Location: Aberdare National Park

Highlights: Karuru Falls is the tallest waterfall in Kenya, cascading down three steps with a combined height of around 273 meters. The lush rainforest and misty scenery make this spot one of the most captivating natural sites in Kenya.

Best Time to Visit: June to October for ideal hiking conditions, as the trails are dryer.

Karuru Falls offers hiking paths that allow travelers to view the falls from various vantage points, making it a rewarding trek for adventure seekers.

Thompson Falls
Location: Nyahururu Town, Laikipia County
Highlights: At 74 meters high, Thompson Falls is a popular spot in central Kenya, set against the backdrop of thick forest and rugged cliffs. Visitors can descend a series of stairs to the base of the falls or enjoy the panoramic view from the top.

Best Time to Visit: Year-round, though early mornings and evenings offer the most tranquil atmosphere.

The falls are named after the explorer Joseph Thompson and are located near Nyahururu, providing an excellent stop for visitors exploring the central highlands.

Fourteen Falls
Location: Near Thika, Kiambu County

Highlights: Fourteen Falls, a series of cascades along the Athi River, is known for its scenic beauty and lush surroundings. The waterfalls offer activities like boat rides, birdwatching, and even cliff diving for the adventurous.

Best Time to Visit: Year-round, with June to October providing ideal weather for exploration.

Fourteen Falls is especially popular among day-trippers and photographers, and the cascading waters provide a beautiful, rhythmic soundtrack for picnics or leisurely strolls.

Lugard Falls
Location: Tsavo East National Park
Highlights: Named after British colonial administrator Sir Frederick Lugard, these falls are unique in that they are more rapids than falls, with turbulent waters flowing through eroded gorges and potholes carved into the rocks. Their unusual rock formations make them a striking sight.

Best Time to Visit: June to October for cooler weather and clearer skies.

Lugard Falls is a great spot to observe crocodiles, which are often seen basking on the rocks nearby.

Gura Falls

Location: Aberdare National Park

Highlights: Gura Falls is one of the most powerful waterfalls in Kenya, set against the lush, forested cliffs of the Aberdare Ranges. With its rugged path and verdant surroundings, Gura is a great place for trekking and photography.

Best Time to Visit: June to October, as trails are less slippery during dry months.

Gura Falls is also part of a scenic area filled with wildlife and is best experienced on a guided trek, as the terrain can be challenging.

Kenya's lakes and waterfalls offer endless opportunities for exploration, from tranquil boat rides on Lake Naivasha to adrenaline-pumping hikes around Karuru Falls. Each destination is a testament to Kenya's natural beauty, providing visitors with both awestruck views and an array of outdoor activities. These aquatic landscapes are perfect for travelers seeking adventure, serenity, or a closer connection to Kenya's rich biodiversity.

Forests and Highlands

Kenya's forests and highlands are ecological treasures, boasting rich biodiversity and stunning landscapes. Among the most celebrated are the Aberdare and Mau Forests, home to lush vegetation, rare animals like the bongo antelope, and an array of bird species. These forests are critical to Kenya's environmental health, serving as water catchment areas for major rivers and providing essential resources for local communities. The Aberdare Ranges, in particular, are a cool, mist-laden region of waterfalls, dense forests, and moorlands, offering both environmental importance and scenic beauty.

The Kenyan highlands, with altitudes ranging from 1,500 to 3,500 meters, are a mix of fertile farmland and protected wilderness. These regions include the Kikuyu and Nyandarua Ranges, where tea and coffee plantations thrive alongside indigenous forests and wildlife sanctuaries. The highlands' cooler climate and fertile volcanic soils make them key agricultural areas, contributing to the country's economy while supporting diverse plant and animal species. Hikers and nature lovers often explore the scenic paths winding through these mountains, offering views of towering cliffs, valleys, and distant peaks.

Together, Kenya's forests and highlands form essential habitats, hosting unique ecosystems and endangered species. These areas are popular for eco-tourism activities, including birdwatching, hiking, and cultural tours with local communities. The mix of highland climate, rich biodiversity, and cultural heritage provides a memorable experience for visitors while underscoring the need for conservation to preserve these natural wonders for future generations.

Desert and Semi-Arid Landscapes

Kenya's desert and semi-arid landscapes offer a stark yet captivating contrast to its lush forests and green highlands. The northern regions, including areas like Turkana, Marsabit, and Samburu, are characterized by vast deserts, rocky plateaus, and sparse vegetation. These landscapes, shaped by millennia of erosion and intense heat, feature remarkable geological formations, like volcanic hills and ancient lava flows, which create an otherworldly aesthetic. This rugged environment is home to resilient communities and unique wildlife, such as Grevy's zebra, Somali ostrich, and oryx, adapted to survive in the arid conditions.

In these regions, local cultures and traditions are deeply tied to the land, with communities like the Turkana, Samburu, and Rendille maintaining traditional pastoralist lifestyles. These communities have adapted to the harsh climate, relying on sustainable practices to manage scarce resources, including water and grazing land. The cultural heritage, reflected in their vibrant dress, music, and crafts, draws visitors interested in cultural tourism, often paired with visits to natural landmarks like Lake Turkana—the world's largest desert lake, known for its surreal beauty and fossil sites.

Kenya's desert and semi-arid landscapes also offer unique adventures for travelers, from camel treks and camping under star-filled skies to exploring the Chalbi Desert's salt flats and Marsabit's green oasis. These arid regions are increasingly popular for eco-tourism, providing opportunities to appreciate Kenya's diverse geography and experience its resilient cultures, and gain insights into the environmental challenges posed by climate change.

Chapter 9
Kenyan Cuisine: A Culinary Journey

Popular Dishes and Street Food

Kenya's popular dishes and street foods capture the heart of its diverse culinary traditions and are integral to daily life across the country. Ugali is a staple dish—made from maize flour and resembling a thick porridge—served alongside vegetables, stews, or nyama choma (grilled meat). Another favorite is sukuma wiki, a simple, flavorful dish of collard greens sautéed with onions, tomatoes, and spices, typically paired with ugali. Among coastal communities, dishes like pilau (spiced rice with meat) and biryani (a fragrant rice dish with a blend of spices) showcase Indian and Arabic influences, while coconut-based curries offer a tropical twist.

Street food is equally beloved, with vendors in towns and cities offering quick, delicious bites that reflect Kenya's vibrant food culture. Samosas, crispy pastries filled with spiced meat or vegetables, and mandazi (lightly sweetened fried dough) are popular snacks enjoyed with tea. Chapati, a soft, layered flatbread, is another staple, often served as a side or enjoyed on its own. Roasted mahindi choma (grilled corn on the cob) is a favorite roadside snack, especially during harvest seasons, while mutura (Kenyan sausage made with seasoned ground meat) brings communities together, often prepared for celebrations.

Kenya's street food also includes refreshing beverages and desserts. In bustling markets, vendors serve sugarcane juice and madafu (coconut water) to cool down in the tropical heat. Sweet treats like kashata (coconut and peanut brittle) and viazi karai (battered and fried potatoes) satisfy sweet and savory cravings alike. For visitors, Kenya's street food scene offers an authentic, flavorful experience, showcasing local ingredients, culinary creativity, and a sense of community that makes it a delightful part of the Kenyan journey.

Fine Dining in Nairobi and Mombasa

Kenya's urban hubs, Nairobi and Mombasa, have blossomed into fine dining destinations, offering culinary experiences that range from high-end local flavors to international fusion. Nairobi, as Kenya's capital and cultural center, is home to acclaimed restaurants that fuse African ingredients with modern gastronomy. Establishments like Talisman and Hemingways Nairobi present refined Kenyan and African-inspired dishes in elegant settings, often incorporating organic, locally sourced ingredients. Carnivore is another iconic venue, famous for its all-you-can-eat meat selection, including exotic options like ostrich and crocodile, all grilled over an open flame.

Mombasa, Kenya's coastal city, is known for its unique blend of Swahili, Arabic, and Indian culinary influences. Fine dining in Mombasa includes establishments like Tamarind Mombasa, a renowned seafood restaurant with stunning ocean views and a menu featuring dishes like crab, prawns, and lobster with coastal spice. Forodhani

Restaurant, located in the Old Town, offers Swahili fine dining with dishes like coconut fish curry, pilau rice, and fresh tropical fruit desserts, all set in the ambiance of historic architecture.

Both Nairobi and Mombasa cater to international palates as well, with fine dining restaurants offering Italian, French, Indian, and Japanese cuisines. For a true fusion experience, Seven Seafood & Grill in Nairobi combines fresh Kenyan seafood with flavors from the Mediterranean and Asia, while Jahazi Grill in Mombasa brings Indian flavors into Swahili dishes. The fine dining scene in these cities not only celebrates Kenya's rich culinary heritage but also showcases its growing global food influence, providing an unforgettable experience for both locals and visitors.

Traditional Kenyan Meals

Traditional Kenyan meals are hearty, flavorful, and rooted in the diverse culinary practices of the country's ethnic communities. At the heart of many Kenyan meals is ugali, a dense maize porridge that serves as a base for various dishes. Ugali is typically paired with sukuma wiki (collard greens cooked) with onions and tomatoes) or rich stews, such as nyama (beef) or chicken stew. This combination is nourishing and affordable, making it a staple in most Kenyan households. Another popular accompaniment to ugali is tilapia, especially near Lake Victoria, where the fish is often fried or grilled and served with kachumbari, a fresh tomato and onion salad.

Among the Kikuyu community, irio is a cherished dish, made by mashing boiled potatoes, green peas, and maize, sometimes with added pumpkin leaves for flavor. The Maasai community's traditional meals reflect their pastoral lifestyle, focusing on milk, meat, and blood from livestock. Their diet often includes mutura, a sausage made with spiced ground meat and blood, which is prepared for special occasions and celebrations.

Kenya's coastal communities contribute a distinct culinary style influenced by Swahili, Indian, and Arabic flavors. Dishes like pilau (spiced rice with meat) and biryani are common, with spices like cardamom, cinnamon, and cloves enhancing the flavor. The coastal people also enjoy coconut-based curries, such as coconut fish curry and maharagwe ya nazi (coconut bean stew), reflecting the availability of tropical ingredients. Traditional Kenyan meals are more than food—they embody the country's cultural diversity, agricultural richness, and communal way of life.

Vegan and Vegetarian Options

Kenya offers a range of delicious vegan and vegetarian options, often rooted in traditional dishes that naturally exclude meat or animal products. A staple for many Kenyans, sukuma wiki—a simple dish made from sautéed collard greens, tomatoes, and onions—is both vegan and widely available. It is typically served with ugali (maize meal) or chapati (unleavened flatbread), creating a filling and nutritious meal. Irio, a Kikuyu dish of mashed potatoes, peas, and corn, is another popular vegetarian option that can be made vegan if prepared without butter.

Coastal Kenyan cuisine offers a variety of vegan and vegetarian dishes rich in spices and tropical ingredients. Maharagwe ya nazi (coconut bean stew) is a beloved coastal dish made with red beans cooked in a flavorful coconut milk base, served over rice or with chapati. Vegetable pilau, a spiced rice dish cooked with ingredients like cardamom, cloves, and cinnamon, can also be enjoyed as a vegan meal when made without ghee or meat. For a savory snack, bhajias (spiced chickpea flour fritters), often served with a side of kachumbari (tomato and onion salad), are a popular street food option.

Many Kenyan street foods are vegan-friendly as well. Vendors across the country offer snacks like mahindi choma (grilled corn on the cob), seasoned with a sprinkle of salt and chili, and samosas filled with spiced vegetables. Fresh tropical fruits, such as mango, pineapple, and papaya, are widely available and make for refreshing vegan treats. Overall, Kenyan cuisine provides an abundance of flavorful vegan and vegetarian options, blending indigenous ingredients with cultural influences that cater to diverse dietary needs.

Chapter 10
Shopping in Kenya

Kenya's shopping scene is a rich fusion of traditional artistry, modern fashion, and culturally inspired souvenirs. From bustling local markets to high-end boutiques, shopping in Kenya offers visitors an authentic taste of the country's heritage and craftsmanship while supporting local artisans and businesses. Whether you're interested in vibrant textiles, unique jewelry, handcrafted home décor, or Kenyan tea and coffee, shopping here provides a memorable experience and a meaningful connection to Kenyan culture.

Kenya's local markets are vibrant, bustling hubs of culture, creativity, and craftsmanship, offering a truly immersive shopping experience for visitors. These markets are where Kenya's artisans showcase a range of traditional handicrafts, from Maasai beadwork to hand-carved wooden sculptures, woven baskets, and colorful fabrics. The Maasai Market, held in Nairobi and rotating locations throughout the week, is a top destination for anyone seeking authentic Kenyan handicrafts. Here, visitors can find intricately beaded jewelry, leather sandals, sisal baskets, and kikoi and kanga fabrics, each telling the story of the artisan's heritage and culture.

Among the standout handicrafts are soapstone carvings from the Kisii community, highly prized for their smooth finish and intricate designs, often depicting wildlife or abstract patterns. Another unique item is Akamba wood carvings, originating from the Akamba community, known for their detailed animal figurines, masks, and household items like bowls and trays. These wood sculptures are meticulously hand-carved and showcase the skill and dedication of Kenyan craftsmen. Similarly, sisal baskets from the Kamba women's cooperatives are popular for their durability and eco-friendly appeal, blending traditional techniques with vibrant colors and patterns.

For travelers interested in supporting sustainable tourism, purchasing these crafts directly from local markets or artisan cooperatives ensures fair wages for artisans and preserves traditional crafts. Beyond souvenirs, these items make meaningful contributions to the lives of artisans and their families, reflecting the beauty, resilience, and creativity of Kenyan culture. Shopping in Kenya's local markets is not just about finding unique souvenirs; it's about connecting with the stories and traditions behind each handmade piece.

Souvenirs to Bring Home

Kenya offers an array of unique souvenirs that capture its rich culture, natural beauty, and skilled craftsmanship, making them perfect mementos to bring home. Among the most popular are Maasai beadwork and jewelry, vibrant pieces that symbolize Maasai heritage and are crafted with intricate patterns and bold colors. These items include bracelets, necklaces, and earrings, each carrying cultural significance and often used in traditional ceremonies. Another must-have souvenir is kanga or kikoi fabric, versatile cloths adorned with colorful designs and Swahili sayings, which can be used as wraps, scarves, or decorative pieces in the home.

Kenya is also known for its soapstone carvings from the Kisii region, which make for stunning decorative pieces. These sculptures, typically depicting animals, abstract art, or everyday scenes, are polished to a smooth finish and come in natural colors like cream, pink, and grey. Akamba wood carvings are another unique souvenir, including beautifully crafted animal figurines, tribal masks, and utility items like bowls and utensils, all highlighting the artistry of Kenya's Akamba craftsmen.

For a taste of Kenya, Kenyan coffee and tea are top choices, renowned worldwide for their rich flavors. Buying these items locally guarantees quality and freshness, with many shops offering premium Arabica coffee beans from Kenya's highlands and black tea from the renowned Kericho region. Additionally, spices from the coastal markets, such as cloves, cardamom, and cinnamon, capture the Swahili influence on Kenyan cuisine and add an exotic touch to home cooking. Each of these souvenirs not only makes for memorable gifts but also supports local artisans and communities, adding meaning to each item brought home from Kenya.

Best Malls and Shopping Centers

Kenya's shopping malls and centers provide a modern shopping experience with a mix of high-end boutiques, local designer stores, restaurants, and entertainment options. In Nairobi, Sarit Centre in Westlands is one of the oldest and most popular malls, known for its wide selection of shops, including both local and international brands, as well as a cinema, food court, and supermarket. Another favorite is Village Market in Gigiri, which combines shopping with leisure activities, featuring art galleries, boutique stores, a bowling alley, and a water park. Village Market also hosts an extensive selection of restaurants offering both local and international cuisine, making it a complete destination for shopping and relaxation.

Westgate Shopping Mall, also in Westlands, is a modern center with a luxurious feel, offering an upscale shopping experience with international brands, Kenyan designer boutiques, and specialty stores. The mall's diverse selection of cafes and restaurants adds to its appeal, attracting both locals and tourists looking for quality shopping and dining options. Two Rivers Mall, located in the Runda area of Nairobi, is East Africa's largest mall and a major attraction for shoppers, housing a vast range of international brands, a theme park, and a variety of entertainment options, including an IMAX theater and outdoor activities.

In Mombasa, City Mall Nyali is a popular shopping destination, offering a mix of retail stores, supermarkets, and eateries. The mall has become a community hub, especially for visitors in the coastal region looking for a relaxed shopping experience close to the beach. Nakumatt Nyali, another prominent shopping center in Mombasa, provides essential retail stores, a supermarket, and a few boutiques, offering convenience for visitors and locals alike. Kenya's malls cater to a variety of tastes and needs, from luxury shopping to family entertainment, providing a memorable shopping experience that blends local culture with global influences.

Bargaining Tips and Tricks

Bargaining is an integral part of shopping in Kenya's markets and smaller shops, especially for souvenirs, handicrafts, and clothing. Here are some key tips and tricks to ensure a smooth and enjoyable bargaining experience:

Do Your Research: Before heading to the market, take some time to research the general prices for items you're interested in. If possible, check with locals or hotel staff to get an idea of fair prices. This will give you a starting point and help you gauge when a price is too high.

Stay Friendly and Polite: Bargaining in Kenya is often done with a friendly, conversational approach. Smile, maintain a positive attitude, and show appreciation for the item. Kenyans value respectful interactions, and a friendly demeanor can go a long way in securing a good deal.

Start Low but Be Reasonable: Begin with a price lower than what you're willing to pay, but avoid offering an amount that may be seen as insulting. From there, negotiate upwards, aiming to meet the seller somewhere in the middle. A good rule of thumb is to start at about 50% of the asking price, though this may vary based on the seller and location.

Be Prepared to Walk Away: Sellers are often willing to lower their prices if they feel they may lose a sale. Politely walking away shows that you're not desperate to buy, which might lead to the seller offering a better price to keep you interested. If they don't lower the price, you can always return if you're still interested.

Buy in Bulk for Better Deals: If you plan to purchase multiple items from one seller, use this as leverage to negotiate a better price. Sellers are more likely to offer a discount if you buy several items, making it a win-win for both parties.

Bring Small Bills: Having smaller denominations on hand is practical for both you and the seller. It allows you to pay the agreed-upon price exactly, and you can politely refuse if a seller claims they "don't have change" as a tactic to raise the price slightly.

Enjoy the Experience: Bargaining in Kenya is not just about getting a good price; it's also a cultural experience. Take time to connect with the sellers, ask about the crafts, and share a laugh. Many sellers take pride in their items, so engaging in conversation shows respect and makes the interaction memorable.

With these tips, you'll be able to bargain effectively and have a richer shopping experience in Kenya's vibrant markets.

Chapter 11
Health and Safety
in Kenya

Vaccinations and Medical Preparations

Traveling to Kenya requires certain vaccinations and medical preparations to ensure a safe and healthy trip. Below is a list of recommended vaccinations, preventative medications, and general health precautions for visitors:

Routine Vaccinations: Ensure that routine vaccines, such as measles-mumps-rubella (MMR), diphtheria-tetanus-pertussis, and influenza, are up to date. This is particularly important for international travel.

Required Vaccinations

Yellow Fever: This vaccine is required for travelers over nine months old if arriving from countries with a risk of yellow fever transmission. Some travelers may also need to show proof of this vaccine upon re-entry to their home country, so it's advised to check requirements well in advance.

Recommended Vaccinations

Typhoid and Hepatitis A: These are recommended for most travelers, as these diseases can be contracted through contaminated food or water.

Hepatitis B: This vaccine is recommended for travelers who may come into close contact with locals or for extended stays, as it can be transmitted through bodily fluids.

Rabies: Kenya has some risk of rabies, especially in rural or wildlife areas where animal contact is possible. This vaccine is recommended for travelers planning extended stays, working with animals, or visiting remote areas.

Malaria Prevention: Malaria is prevalent in many regions of Kenya, particularly in lower-altitude and coastal areas. Travelers are advised to take antimalarial medication as prescribed by their healthcare provider. Options include atovaquone-proguanil, doxycycline, or mefloquine, based on individual needs and health history. It's also wise to use insect repellent, wear long sleeves, and sleep under a mosquito net, particularly in malaria-prone areas.

Other Health Precautions

Traveler's Diarrhea: Carry a small supply of medications for traveler's diarrhea, like loperamide or antibiotics, which can be useful if prescribed by a doctor.

Water Safety: Stick to bottled or boiled water to avoid waterborne diseases. Avoid ice and fresh juices from unknown sources, as these may be made with untreated water.

Sun Protection: Kenya's sun can be intense, particularly near the equator. High-SPF sunscreen, sunglasses, and a wide-brimmed hat are essential for protection from UV exposure.

COVID-19 Considerations: Although requirements may vary, stay informed about COVID-19 vaccination or testing requirements for entry, which can change based on global health updates.

Travel Insurance: Comprehensive travel insurance that includes coverage for medical evacuation is highly recommended, as some regions may have limited medical facilities.

By making these medical preparations, travelers can enjoy Kenya with peace of mind, staying healthy and well-prepared for a memorable trip.

Safe Travel Tips

Traveling safely in Kenya requires a combination of preparation, awareness, and respect for local customs. Here are some practical safety tips to ensure a smooth and enjoyable journey:

Stay Informed and Plan Ahead: Check travel advisories and the latest updates on safety conditions in Kenya before your trip, particularly in regions with known security risks. Register with your country's embassy in Kenya, especially if you're traveling to remote or rural areas, so they can provide assistance if needed.

Use Trusted Transportation: Use reputable taxi services, such as those recommended by your hotel or through a reliable app like Uber, and avoid unregistered taxis. If you're renting a car, choose a well-established company and avoid driving at night, as some areas have poorly lit roads, wildlife crossings, and unmarked hazards.

Be Cautious with Valuables: In crowded places like markets, malls, and public transportation, keep valuables out of sight and secure. Avoid displaying expensive items, like jewelry, and carry only what you need. A money belt or hidden pouch can help keep cash, passport, and cards secure.

Stay in Safe Areas: In cities like Nairobi and Mombasa, certain neighborhoods are safer than others. Research accommodations in secure areas, and check with your hotel or host about which neighborhoods or areas to avoid, particularly after dark. Many tourist spots have a strong security presence, but remaining vigilant is always wise.

Health and Hygiene Precautions: Stick to bottled or filtered water, avoid ice from unknown sources, and wash your hands frequently, especially before meals. Additionally, apply mosquito repellent and sleep under a mosquito net in malaria-prone areas. Carry a small first-aid kit, including hand sanitizer, bandages, and basic medications for unexpected situations.

Respect Wildlife Safety Rules: If you're going on a safari or visiting natural reserves, always follow the guidance of your tour guides. Keep a safe distance from animals, remain in designated areas, and never attempt to feed or touch wildlife. Wildlife behavior can be unpredictable, so respecting these rules ensures both your safety and the animals' well-being.

Avoid Political Gatherings: Kenya occasionally experiences political rallies or protests, particularly around election periods. Avoid such gatherings, as they can become unpredictable. Keep updated on local news and follow the advice of local authorities and your hotel staff about areas to avoid.

Be Mindful of Cultural Etiquette: Kenyans are generally welcoming, but it's essential to show respect for local customs. Dress modestly in rural and conservative areas, ask for permission before taking photos of locals, and greet people politely. Small gestures of respect can enhance your interactions and keep your travels smooth.

Emergency Contacts and Travel Insurance: Keep a list of emergency contacts, including your country's embassy, local hospitals, and emergency services. Comprehensive travel insurance is highly recommended, covering health care, accidents, and medical evacuation if needed.

By following these safety tips, you can make the most of your time in Kenya, exploring its beautiful landscapes and vibrant culture with confidence and peace of mind.

Navigating Kenyan Cities Safely

Navigating Kenyan cities, particularly Nairobi and Mombasa, can be an exciting experience, but it's essential to stay vigilant and prepared to ensure your safety. Here are some practical tips for navigating the cities safely:

Use Trusted Transport Options

Taxis and Ride-Hailing: Opt for reputable taxi services or use ride-hailing apps like Uber and Bolt, which are widely available in cities like Nairobi and Mombasa. These services allow you to track your journey and offer a safer alternative to hailing a taxi off the street. Always confirm the vehicle details before getting in.

Public Transport: Public buses and matatus (shared minivans) are commonly used but can be crowded, unregulated, and prone to reckless driving. If you decide to use them, exercise caution, especially during peak hours. It's advisable to take matatus only if you're familiar with the route or travel with locals who know the area.

Walking: In areas like Nairobi's city center, walking is possible, but it's best to avoid walking in unfamiliar or poorly lit areas at night. Stick to busy, well-lit streets and avoid side streets, especially after dark.

Stay Alert in Crowded Areas

Pickpocketing: In crowded markets, bus stations, or public events, be mindful of your belongings. Pickpockets are common in busy areas. Use a money belt or a cross-body bag, and avoid carrying too much cash or valuables. Keep your phone, wallet, and passport in a secure, hidden place.

Avoid Distractions: While exploring, avoid distractions like looking at your phone or carrying large bags that could attract unwanted attention. Stay aware of your surroundings and avoid talking to strangers who might try to engage you in a scam or distraction.

Choose Safe Accommodations

Location: Choose accommodations in safer neighborhoods with good reputations, such as Westlands, Karen, or Gigiri in Nairobi, or Nyali in Mombasa. Research the area and consult your hotel staff for guidance on which districts are safer to explore.

Hotel Security: Make sure your hotel has adequate security measures, such as 24-hour reception, security guards, and secure entry points. Always lock your doors and windows when inside your room and avoid leaving valuables unattended.

Avoid Risky Areas After Dark

Nighttime Safety: In both Nairobi and Mombasa, some neighborhoods can be dangerous after dark, with higher risks of crime. Stick to well-lit, busy areas in the evening and avoid walking alone in unfamiliar areas. If you must travel after dark, use a trusted taxi or ride-hailing service.

Avoid Walking in Secluded Areas: Avoid walking through secluded or poorly lit areas, such as alleyways or residential backstreets, especially if you're unfamiliar with the area. Always try to travel in groups or with locals who know the area well.

Be Cautious with Street Vendors and Beggars

Street Vendors: While street vendors sell everything from snacks to souvenirs, they can sometimes be overly persistent. It's best to politely decline if you're not interested in buying. Bargaining is common, but always remain firm and respectful when negotiating prices.

Beggars: While many people in cities may approach you for money, it's advisable not to give money directly to beggars. Instead, consider donating to local charities or purchasing goods from vendors as an alternative way to help.

Know Emergency Contacts

Police and Emergency Services: Familiarize yourself with the emergency contact numbers for police, ambulances, and fire services. In Kenya, dial 999 or 112 for emergency services.

Embassy Contact: It's helpful to have the contact information for your country's embassy or consulate in case of emergencies. Keep a hard copy of important documents, such as your passport and travel insurance details, in case they are lost or stolen.

Be Aware of Traffic and Road Conditions

Road Safety: Kenyan traffic can be chaotic, and driving standards vary. If you plan on driving, ensure you're familiar with local road rules and signs. Many roads in Nairobi and other cities can be congested, especially during rush hours (morning and evening). Always be cautious when crossing streets, as pedestrian crossings are often ignored by vehicles.

Avoid Road Rage: Avoid engaging in arguments or confrontations with local drivers, as road rage can escalate quickly. If you're traveling by car, always use seat belts and follow traffic rules.

Stay Hydrated and Protect Yourself from the Sun

Water Safety: Drink bottled or filtered water to avoid waterborne diseases, especially if you're in urban areas. Always check that the seal on bottled water is intact before drinking.

Sun Protection: The sun can be intense in Kenya, particularly near the equator. Wear sunscreen with a high SPF, a hat, and sunglasses to protect yourself from the sun's harmful UV rays.

By following these tips, you can navigate Kenyan cities more safely and confidently, allowing you to focus on enjoying the vibrant culture and attractions Kenya has to offer. Stay aware, stay alert, and take basic precautions to ensure a smooth and safe experience.

Emergency Contacts and Services

In case of an emergency while in Kenya, it's important to have access to key contacts and services. Here's a list of critical emergency contacts and services to help ensure your safety and peace of mind during your trip:

- **Emergency Numbers**

Police: Dial 999 or 112 for police assistance in case of theft, accidents, or emergencies.

Ambulance/Medical Emergency: Dial 999 or 112 for ambulance services. Many hospitals also have direct emergency lines, which may be helpful to note.

Fire Services: Dial 999 or 112 for fire emergencies.

National Disaster Management Unit: 020 234 2001 – For large-scale emergencies like natural disasters or accidents involving multiple parties.

- **Medical Assistance**

Nairobi Hospital: One of the top hospitals in Kenya with excellent emergency and trauma care.

Contact: +254 20 272 6300 or +254 724 256 700

Aga Khan University Hospital Nairobi: A major hospital offering high-quality healthcare services, including emergency care.

Contact: +254 20 366 2000 or +254 722 205 970

Mombasa Hospital: For emergency medical care in Mombasa.

Contact: +254 41 222 4171

Karen Hospital (Nairobi): A well-known healthcare provider with a comprehensive emergency department.

Contact: +254 20 210 9060

- **Embassy Contacts**

U.S. Embassy Nairobi: For U.S. citizens, the embassy can provide assistance in emergencies, such as loss of passport, legal issues, or natural disasters.

Contact: +254 20 363 6450 (24/7) or +254 20 363 6000 Address: United States Embassy, Nairobi, Kenya.

British High Commission Nairobi: For UK citizens, the high commission can assist with consular services in an emergency.

Contact: +254 20 288 6000 or +254 731 104 300 Address: British High Commission, Nairobi, Kenya.

Australian High Commission Nairobi: For Australian citizens needing assistance in an emergency.

Contact: +254 20 423 4000 or +254 713 071 194 Address: Australian High Commission, Nairobi, Kenya.

- **Emergency Services for Specific Regions**

Coast Guard: For emergencies along the coastline, such as accidents or boat-related issues.

Contact: +254 20 800 2145

Wildlife Emergencies (Poaching or Animal Attacks):

Kenya Wildlife Service (KWS): +254 20 600 8000 or +254 727 732 124

Anti-Poaching Unit: +254 722 777 005

- **Security & Safety Services**

Private Security Companies: In case of security concerns or threats, you can contact private security providers in cities like Nairobi or Mombasa. Some trusted companies include G4S Kenya (+254 20 338 2345) or KK Security (+254 20 351 5175).

Tourism Police: In major tourist areas, such as Nairobi, Mombasa, and national parks, the Tourist Police Unit is dedicated to assisting travelers.

Contact: +254 20 213 7711 or +254 717 555 555

- **Lost Passport or Travel Document Assistance**

Consular Services: If you lose your passport or travel documents, contact your country's embassy or consulate immediately for assistance with replacements.

Lost Property: For lost luggage or personal items, contact your airline directly or visit the local police station to file a report.

- **Travel Insurance and Medical Evacuation**

Travel Insurance: Ensure you have comprehensive travel insurance that covers medical treatment, emergency evacuation, and lost luggage. Most providers have 24/7 emergency hotlines that you can call for assistance while in Kenya.

Medical Evacuation: In case of serious health emergencies, Kenya has medical evacuation services, often coordinated through travel insurance providers. You can also contact specialized air ambulance services like Flying Doctors:

Contact: +254 20 603 435 or +254 731 616 161

- **Useful Local Numbers**

Road Safety and Traffic Accidents: For accidents or breakdowns, contact Kenya Red Cross at +254 20 273 4900 or +254 733 333 030 for assistance.

Water and Power Issues: For any emergency related to water or electricity, contact Kenya Power (+254 711 011 111) or Nairobi Water & Sewerage Company (+254 20 355 5657).

- **Communication with Locals**

Language: While English is widely spoken in Kenya, knowing a few phrases in Swahili, the national language, can be helpful in emergencies. Common phrases like "Nisaidie" (Help me) or "Poa" (Okay/It's fine) can assist in communicating in distress situations.

- **General Tips for Emergencies**

Carry Copies of Your Important Documents: Keep photocopies of your passport, visa, travel insurance, and emergency contacts in a safe place, separate from your originals.

Stay Calm: In emergencies, staying calm and following instructions can be crucial. Always provide clear information to emergency services about your location and the nature of the emergency.

Know Your Location: Whether you're in a city or on safari, always be aware of your surroundings and know the nearest landmarks, hotel, or facility you can contact for help.

Having these emergency contacts and services at your fingertips will help ensure that you're prepared in case of an unexpected situation during your travels in Kenya.

Chapter 12
Kenya for Families

Kenya is an excellent destination for family travel, offering a rich blend of natural beauty, wildlife, cultural experiences, and outdoor adventures that appeal to travelers of all ages. Whether you're traveling with young children or teenagers, there are plenty of family-friendly activities and destinations to enjoy together. Here's a guide to make your family trip to Kenya safe, fun, and unforgettable:

Family-Friendly Destinations

Kenya is a fantastic family-friendly destination, offering a wide variety of experiences that cater to all ages. Wildlife enthusiasts can enjoy safari adventures in iconic parks like Maasai Mara and Amboseli National Park, where families can witness the "Big Five" and other wildlife in their natural habitat. The Nairobi National Park, located just outside the city, provides a convenient and unique safari experience with the city skyline as a backdrop, while Tsavo and Lake Naivasha offer quieter, less crowded alternatives perfect for families looking for a peaceful nature escape.

For those seeking a more relaxed holiday, Kenya's beautiful beaches, such as Diani Beach and Watamu, offer pristine coastlines and family-oriented resorts with water sports, snorkeling, and dolphin watching. Mombasa, with its historical sites like Fort Jesus and vibrant coastal atmosphere, is ideal for families interested in culture and history. Lamu Island, with its car-free streets and rich cultural heritage, provides a calm, educational environment for families to explore together.

Additionally, Kenya offers numerous family-friendly activities beyond safaris and beaches. The Giraffe Centre and Karen Blixen Museum in Nairobi provide interactive educational experiences, while places like Hell's Gate National Park and Mount Kenya offer outdoor adventures like hiking and cycling. With a combination of wildlife, cultural exploration, beach relaxation, outdoor activities, Kenya is an ideal destination for creating unforgettable family memories.

Safari with Kids

A safari with kids in Kenya can be an exciting and educational adventure for the entire family. Many safari lodges and tour operators offer kid-friendly experiences that make the journey enjoyable and comfortable. Game drives are often tailored to children's attention spans, with shorter outings and opportunities to spot wildlife like elephants, giraffes, and lions. Some parks, such as Maasai Mara, Amboseli, and Tsavo, provide private game drives, allowing families to explore at their own pace while learning about animal behaviors, conservation, and the natural environment.

In addition to traditional game drives, Kenya's national parks and reserves offer family-friendly activities such as nature walks, bushcraft lessons, and visits to local Maasai villages, where children can engage with indigenous cultures and learn about daily life. Lodges in these areas often feature family suites, swimming pools, and children's programs that keep younger travelers entertained when not on safari. Many accommodations also offer kid-focused amenities like educational talks and even "junior ranger" programs to engage children in learning about wildlife and conservation efforts.

For families with younger children, safaris can be planned with their comfort and safety in mind, with easy access to amenities and the option of combining safari adventures with beach vacations on Kenya's stunning coast. By balancing shorter game drives with relaxation time and family-friendly experiences, a safari in Kenya can be both thrilling and manageable for families of all ages. Whether observing animals on a game drive or learning about conservation, a safari in Kenya offers children a unique opportunity to connect with nature in an unforgettable way.

Best Outdoor Activities for Children

Kenya offers a range of outdoor activities that are perfect for children, allowing them to connect with nature and enjoy thrilling adventures. Safari game drives are a top choice, where kids can spot wildlife like elephants, lions, and zebras in their natural habitats. Family-friendly lodges in parks such as Maasai Mara and Tsavo offer shorter drives and educational commentary, making the experience both exciting and informative for younger travelers.

Nature walks and bushcraft lessons also provide engaging opportunities for children to explore the environment. Guided walks in national parks like Maasai Mara teach kids about local flora and fauna, while bushcraft lessons give them hands-on experiences such as animal tracking and survival skills. Visits to wildlife sanctuaries like the David Sheldrick Wildlife Trust and the Giraffe Centre offer interactive experiences with endangered species, deepening children's understanding of conservation.

For families looking for a mix of adventure and relaxation, Kenya's beaches provide plenty of opportunities for water activities like snorkeling, kayaking, and sandcastle building. Cycling and hiking trips in places like Hell's Gate National Park and Mount Kenya allow children to explore scenic landscapes and wildlife. Cultural activities, such as visits to local Maasai communities, offer children the chance to learn about Kenya's traditions through interactive experiences, making it a well-rounded destination for outdoor fun and education.

Educational Experiences and Cultural Programs

Kenya offers a rich variety of educational experiences and cultural programs that provide children and families with opportunities to learn about wildlife, conservation, and local traditions. Many wildlife conservation centers, like the David Sheldrick Wildlife Trust and the Giraffe Centre, provide educational programs where children can interact with endangered animals like elephants and giraffes, learning about the importance of conservation and the efforts to protect these species. These experiences help foster a deeper appreciation for wildlife and environmental protection.

In addition to wildlife education, Kenya's cultural programs offer insight into the traditions and lifestyles of its diverse ethnic groups. Families can visit local Maasai, Samburu, and Kikuyu villages to learn about their history, customs, and daily life. Children can participate in cultural activities like traditional dances, bead-making, and craft workshops, offering a hands-on way to experience Kenya's cultural diversity. These interactions allow children to gain a greater understanding of the country's rich heritage and the value of preserving cultural traditions.

Kenya also offers educational opportunities in its museums and historical sites. The Karen Blixen Museum and Fort Jesus in Mombasa provide a glimpse into Kenya's colonial history, while the National Museums of Kenya in Nairobi showcase exhibits on natural history, archaeology, and Kenyan culture. These museums are excellent for families looking to expand their knowledge of Kenya's past and the rich cultural tapestry that has shaped the nation today. Through these educational experiences, children and families can gain a well-rounded understanding of Kenya's history, culture, and wildlife.

Chapter 13
Frequently Asked Questions

Common Queries for First-Time Visitors

What should I know before my first visit to Kenya?

Before visiting Kenya, it's important to understand the country's diverse geography, ranging from savannahs and forests to coastal areas and highlands. Be prepared for varied climates depending on where you're visiting—coastal areas can be hot and humid, while the highlands may be cooler. It's also helpful to be aware of the different cultural practices, as Kenya is home to over 40 ethnic groups, each with unique traditions.

How long should I stay in Kenya for a good experience?

For a well-rounded Kenyan experience, a trip of 7 to 10 days is ideal. This allows time for safaris in multiple parks (e.g., Maasai Mara, Amboseli,

Tsavo), a visit to Nairobi, and some time to relax on the coast. If you have more time, you can explore further destinations like Mount Kenya or Lamu Island.

How can I get around Kenya?

Getting around Kenya is fairly easy, with various transportation options including domestic flights, taxis, public buses, and car hire. For safaris, most visitors opt for guided tours, as they offer convenience and expert knowledge. While there are good road networks, some rural areas may have rough roads, so a 4x4 vehicle is often recommended.

What is the local cuisine like?

Kenyan cuisine is diverse, with influences from indigenous communities as well as Indian and Arab traders. Staple foods include ugali (maize porridge), sukuma (collard greens), and nyama choma (grilled meat). Street food, such as samosas and mangos, is also popular. If you're a foodie, make sure to try local delicacies like Nyama choma, chapati, and githeri (a mixed dish of beans and maize).

Do I need travel insurance for my trip to Kenya?

It is highly recommended to have travel insurance when visiting Kenya. Insurance should cover medical emergencies, lost luggage, flight cancellations, and unexpected situations. In case you're planning on going on a safari or adventure activities like hiking, make sure your insurance includes coverage for those activities.

Is tipping customary in Kenya?

Yes, tipping is common in Kenya, especially in the service industry. While not obligatory, it's customary to leave tips for tour guides, safari drivers, hotel staff, and restaurant workers. For example, a 10% to 15% tip for good service in restaurants is appreciated, and for safari guides, around $10 to $20 per day is a good guideline.

What is the internet and Wi-Fi situation in Kenya?

Internet access in Kenya is fairly widespread, especially in major cities like Nairobi and Mombasa. Hotels, cafes, and restaurants in urban areas often offer free Wi-Fi. However, in remote areas, internet connectivity may be limited. Purchasing a local SIM card with data is a good option for staying connected, and major mobile networks like Safaricom and Airtel offer affordable data packages.

Is it safe to walk around in Kenyan cities?

While urban areas like Nairobi and Mombasa are generally safe, it's advisable to stay cautious, especially in unfamiliar neighborhoods. Stick to well-lit, busy areas at night and avoid walking alone after dark. Using reputable taxis or rideshare apps like Uber can provide extra security. In rural areas, locals are generally friendly, but be mindful of your surroundings.

What cultural norms should I be aware of?

Respect for local traditions is important in Kenya. In rural areas, it's best to dress modestly, especially when visiting religious sites or villages. Handshakes are common greetings, and it's polite to greet people when entering shops, lodges, or restaurants. Also, while Kenyans are generally friendly, it's considered respectful to ask for permission before photographing people, especially in indigenous communities.

What is the best way to handle money in Kenya?

The Kenyan Shilling (KES) is the local currency, and it's recommended to carry cash for smaller purchases, particularly in rural areas. ATMs are widely available in urban centers, and most hotels and larger establishments accept credit cards. However, it's still a good idea to carry some cash for small markets and local vendors. Mobile money services like M-Pesa are popular and widely used for transactions.

Are safaris suitable for first-time visitors?

Yes, safaris in Kenya are well-suited for first-time visitors. There are a variety of safari options ranging from luxury lodges to more budget-friendly camps. The Masai Mara and Amboseli National Park are particularly popular with first-time visitors due to their abundance of wildlife and stunning landscapes. Many tour operators offer guided safari packages tailored to beginners, with knowledgeable guides to ensure an enriching experience.

What should I pack for a trip to Kenya?

When packing for Kenya, focus on light, comfortable clothing, especially for safaris and outdoor activities. Neutral-colored clothes are best for game drives to blend in with the environment. Don't forget essentials like sunscreen, hats, sunglasses, insect repellent, and a camera. If you plan to visit the beach, pack swimwear, light clothing, and flip-flops. A good pair of hiking shoes is also useful if you plan on exploring Kenya's scenic landscapes.

Kenya Travel Do's and Don'ts

Do's

★ Do Respect Local Customs and Traditions Kenya is a diverse country with over 40 ethnic groups, each with unique customs. Be mindful of local cultural practices, particularly in rural areas. When visiting villages, it's respectful to ask permission before taking photos of people or their homes.

★ Do Stay Hydrated The climate in Kenya can vary from hot and humid on the coast to cooler temperatures in the highlands, so it's important to drink plenty of water, especially when traveling on safari or hiking. Always opt for bottled water, as tap water is not safe to drink.

★ Do Use Reputable Transportation For safety, use trusted transportation options like registered taxis or rideshare services such as Uber in urban areas. If you plan to rent a car, choose a reliable agency and ensure your vehicle is suitable for the terrain, especially if you're visiting rural or remote areas.

★ Do Carry Cash and Cards While major cities and tourist spots often accept credit cards, smaller towns and rural areas may require cash. It's advisable to carry a combination of cash (in Kenyan Shillings) and a card, especially for markets, local shops, and taxis.

★ Do Respect Wildlife and Nature Kenya's wildlife is one of its most treasured assets. Always follow the rules set by park authorities, stay in vehicles during game drives, and avoid disturbing animals. Maintain a safe distance and never feed wildlife, as it can be harmful to both you and the animals.

★ Do Tip for Good Service Tipping is appreciated in Kenya, especially for hotel staff, tour guides, safari drivers, and restaurant workers. Generally, 10-15% in restaurants and around $10-20 per day for safari guides is considered appropriate.

★ Do Stay Informed About Health and Safety It's crucial to stay updated on vaccinations and any health precautions. Malaria is present in some areas, so consider taking prophylactic medications and always carry insect repellent. Travel insurance is also highly recommended.

★ Do Embrace the Local Cuisine Kenyan food is delicious and diverse, from nyama choma (grilled meat) to ugali (maize porridge). Be adventurous and try local dishes, but also be cautious with street food to avoid stomach issues.

Don'ts

❖ Don't Engage in Negative Behavior Toward Locals Be respectful towards the Kenyan people, who are known for their friendliness and hospitality. Avoid being condescending or dismissive of local traditions, particularly when visiting rural communities or religious sites.

❖ Don't Point at People In Kenyan culture, pointing at people can be seen as rude, especially in rural communities. If you need to indicate something, use your whole hand or gesture politely.

❖ Don't Walk Around at Night in Unfamiliar Areas While many places in Kenya are safe, it's best to avoid walking around at night, especially in unfamiliar or poorly lit areas. Stick to well-lit, busy streets, and always use reputable taxis or rideshares after dark.

❖ Don't Engage in Bargaining Aggressively Bargaining is common in markets and with street vendors, but it should be done politely and with a smile. Don't haggle aggressively or be disrespectful if you're unable to agree on a price. It's part of the local culture, but mutual respect is important.

❖ Don't Take Photos Without Asking Permission Always ask for permission before photographing people, particularly in indigenous communities like the Maasai or Samburu. In some areas, photography may be prohibited, and it's important to be respectful of people's privacy.

❖ Don't Forget to Protect Against Mosquitoes Malaria is a risk in some areas, particularly in coastal and lowland regions. Always use insect repellent, sleep under a mosquito net, and wear long sleeves and pants in the evenings to avoid bites.

- ❖ Don't Litter or Pollute the Environment Kenya's natural beauty is one of its greatest assets, and it's important to preserve it. Always dispose of waste in designated bins and avoid leaving trash behind in national parks, beaches, or wildlife reserves.

- ❖ Don't Drink Tap Water Tap water in Kenya is generally not safe to drink. Always opt for bottled or filtered water, which is widely available at hotels, stores, and restaurants.

By following these do's and don'ts, travelers can have a safe, respectful, and enjoyable trip to Kenya while contributing positively to the local culture and environment.

Chapter 14
Language Tips: Swahili
Phrases for Tourists

Swahili (Kiswahili) is one of Kenya's official
languages and is widely spoken across the country.
While English is commonly used in urban areas and
by many people in the tourism industry, knowing
some basic Swahili phrases can enhance your
experience and help you connect with locals. Here
are some essential Swahili phrases for tourists:

Basic Greetings

Jambo! – Hello! (Informal greeting)

Habari! – How are you? / What's the news?

Response: Nzuri – Good / Fine.

Hujambo? – How are you? (To a single person)

Response: Sijambo – I'm fine.

Shikamoo – A respectful greeting to elders (literally
means "I hold your feet")

Response: Marahaba – I acknowledge you.

Salama – Peace / Safe (used as a greeting or farewell)

Common Phrases

Asante – Thank you

Asante sana – Thank you very much

Karibu – Welcome

Karibu sana – You're very welcome

Pole – I'm sorry / Condolences

Tafadhali – Please

Samahani – Excuse me / Sorry

Hapana – No

Ndio – Yes

Polite Expressions

Habari za asubuhi – Good morning

Habari za jioni – Good evening

Lala salama – Sleep well (Good night)

Kwaharini – Goodbye (more formal, used when someone is leaving)

Tutaonana baadaye – See you later

Useful Travel Phrases

Nahitaji msaada – I need help

Nina furaha kuwa hapa – I'm happy to be here

Unaweza kusema Kiingereza? – Can you speak English?

Niko lost – I'm lost

Maji – Water

Pesa – Money

Bila pesa – No money

Poa – Cool / Okay (informal)

Shopping and Bargaining

Bei gani? – How much is this?

Punguza bei: Reduce the price (used for bargaining)

Nashukuru: I'm grateful

Hii ni nzuri, this is good

Nataka hii, I want this

Directions and Transportation

Wapi [place]? Where is [place]?

Nataka kwenda [place]: I want to go to [place]

Shika upande wa kulia: Take the right side

Shika upande wa kushoto – Take the left side

Basi-Bus

Teksi-Taxi

Kuna [place] karibu? – Is there [place] nearby?

Safety and Emergencies

Tafadhali nipeleke hospitalini: Please take me to the hospital

Nahitaji polisi—I need the police

Msaada! – Help!

Time and Date

Sasa ni saa ngapi? – What time is it now?

Leo ni [day of the week]: Today is [day of the week]

Kesho: Tomorrow

Jana: Yesterday

Numbers

Moja: One

Mbili: Two

Tatu: Three

Nne - Four

Tano: Five

Kumi – Ten

Learning these simple phrases can greatly enhance your trip to Kenya, helping you communicate and connect with locals in a meaningful way. While most Kenyans in urban areas speak English fluently, showing respect for the local language is always appreciated.

Money Matters: Currency and Payment Methods in Kenya

When traveling to Kenya, understanding the local currency and payment methods is essential for a smooth experience. Here's a breakdown of the key money matters to keep in mind:

Kenyan Currency

Currency: The official currency of Kenya is the Kenyan Shilling (KES). It is abbreviated as KSh and comes in both coins and banknotes.

Coins: The coins are available in denominations of 1, 5, 10, 20, and 40 shillings.

Banknotes: The banknotes come in 50, 100, 200, 500, and 1,000 shillings denominations.

Exchanging Currency: Foreign currencies, such as US dollars, Euros, and British pounds, can be exchanged at banks, forex bureaus, and airports. It's advisable to carry US dollars in cash, as it is the easiest foreign currency to exchange, especially in larger cities or for safaris and tours.

ATMs: ATMs are widely available in major cities and tourist destinations. They typically offer cash in Kenyan Shillings. International credit and debit cards (such as Visa and MasterCard) are accepted at many ATMs, but always check for any withdrawal limits and fees.

Payment Methods

Cash: Cash is widely used in Kenya, particularly in local markets, rural areas, and smaller businesses. It's recommended to carry some cash for small transactions, especially in places that don't accept cards.

Credit and Debit Cards: Major credit and debit cards (Visa, MasterCard, and occasionally American Express) are accepted in larger establishments like hotels, restaurants, and some shops. However, card acceptance is limited in smaller businesses and rural areas, so it's wise to always have cash on hand when traveling outside major cities.

Mobile Money: Mobile money services are incredibly popular in Kenya, particularly M-Pesa. This service allows users to send money, pay bills, transfer funds and purchase goods directly via mobile phones. M-Pay is widely accepted for payments in many areas, including shops, taxis, and restaurants. You can easily exchange your cash for M-Pesa credits at local agents, making it a convenient option for daily transactions.

Exchanging Currency

Banks: Currency exchange services are available at major banks throughout Kenya. However, they may have more restrictive operating hours and offer less competitive rates compared to forex bureaus.

Forex Bureaus: Forex bureaus are plentiful in urban areas like Nairobi and Mombasa and offer more competitive exchange rates than banks. They typically charge lower fees and are open later, which makes them more convenient for travelers.

Currency Exchange Rates: Exchange rates fluctuate, so it's always a good idea to compare rates before exchanging large sums of money. Keep an eye on the current exchange rate and be mindful of any hidden fees or unfavorable rates at exchange points.

Tipping and Gratuity

Tipping: Tipping is appreciated in Kenya, particularly in the tourism and hospitality industries. While it is not mandatory, leaving a tip for good service is customary.

Hotels and Lodges: Tip hotel staff and housekeeping approximately KSh 100-200 per night.

Restaurants: In many restaurants, a service charge of 10-15% is automatically added to your bill, but it's still customary to leave an additional tip of 10% for exceptional service.

Safari Guides and Drivers: For safari guides, a tip of $10-20 per day per person is standard, depending on the level of service.

Bargaining

Marketplaces and street vendors: Bargaining is common in Kenyan markets, especially for items like crafts, clothes, and souvenirs. It's typically expected, but make sure to negotiate politely and with respect.

Suggested Tip: When bargaining, start at about 50-60% of the price offered and work your way up, but don't go too low, as it may be seen as disrespectful.

Other Payment Considerations

Exchange Rate Fluctuations: Keep in mind that exchange rates can fluctuate, so it's advisable to check rates before exchanging large sums of money. This can be done online or by asking at forex bureaus.

Travel Cards: Some international travelers use prepaid travel cards, such as Revolut or Wise (formerly TransferWise), to withdraw money from ATMs in Kenya. These cards typically offer favorable exchange rates and low transaction fees, though you'll need to ensure they're accepted in local ATMs.

Safety Tips for Handling Money

Keep Cash Safe: When carrying large amounts of cash, use a money belt or a hotel safe to keep it secure. It's also advisable to carry cash in small denominations for easier transactions.

Beware of Scams: Always be cautious when withdrawing money from ATMs in public places. Stick to ATMs inside banks or shopping centers for added security, and never share your PIN number with anyone.

By understanding Kenya's currency and payment methods, you can ensure smooth financial transactions during your trip and avoid any unexpected hassles. Always carry a mix of payment options to ensure flexibility, particularly if you venture to more remote regions where card payment may not be available.

Chapter 15
Kenya in 2025: What's New?

Kenya's tourism industry is evolving rapidly, and 2025 promises exciting developments for travelers. One of the biggest changes is Kenya's new visa-free entry policy, which eliminates the need for traditional visas for citizens of over 75 countries. This system is replaced by an Electronic Travel Authorization (ETA), streamlining the process for international travelers while maintaining border security. With this shift, Kenya aims to simplify travel and increase tourist arrivals, capitalizing on its rich natural beauty and wildlife attractions

In addition to the ease of entry, Kenya's tourism industry has been on a strong recovery trajectory, with 2023 seeing a significant boost in visitor numbers, exceeding pre-pandemic figures. This positive momentum continues as the country expects to welcome even more visitors in 2024 and beyond. The rise in international interest is attributed to Kenya's unmatched wildlife safaris, pristine beaches, and thriving cultural experiences

Moreover, Kenya is diversifying its offerings with new luxury lodges and enhanced tourist experiences. For instance, luxury properties like the JW Marriott Masai Mara Safari Lodge, opened in late 2023, are drawing more high-end travelers to Kenya's national parks. The tourism sector is set to grow further as new connections, such as increased flight frequencies to popular destinations and collaborations with global airlines like Kenya Airways, improve access to the country

New Hotels, Restaurants, and Attractions

Kenya's tourism and hospitality sector is experiencing significant growth, with 31 new hotels slated to open in 2025, adding thousands of rooms to meet rising visitor demand. These developments include international luxury brands like JW Marriott, which recently opened its first Nairobi property, bringing a 35-story hotel to the city's skyline. Other major hotel chains such as Hyatt and Glee are also expanding, with properties planned in high-demand areas like Westlands and along Nairobi's Northern Bypass

This surge in hotel construction is part of a broader trend that reflects Kenya's ambition to become a premier global tourism hub. The influx of international investment is not only enhancing Kenya's infrastructure but also creating jobs in construction and hospitality. As more tourists flock to the country, these hotels will cater to a wide range of visitors, from eco-conscious travelers seeking sustainable stays to those looking for luxury safaris and city experiences

Alongside the hotel openings, Kenya's expanding tourism offerings include new attractions and services, reinforcing its status as a top African destination. This growing infrastructure will provide visitors with world-class experiences in both Nairobi and other key tourist hubs, supporting Kenya's economic growth and positioning it as a significant player in global tourism.

Updated Travel Regulations

In 2025, Kenya has introduced several updates to its travel regulations that travelers need to be aware of. One significant change is the introduction of the Electronic Travel Authorization (ETA) system, replacing traditional visas for many nationalities. While nationals from East African Community countries do not need an ETA, travelers from other countries must apply online before their trip. The ETA costs around USD 30 and is processed within three business days

Health and vaccination requirements also remain a key part of travel preparations. Travelers from yellow fever-endemic areas must show proof of yellow fever vaccination at least 10 days before their arrival. Malaria precautions are recommended for those visiting areas like the coast or Rift Valley, and vaccines for typhoid, hepatitis A, and B are strongly advised. Some COVID-19 regulations may still be in place, including proof of vaccination or a negative PCR test, depending on the current situation

For convenience, travelers can rely on mobile payment systems like Pesa, especially in urban areas, as well as cash for transactions in rural regions. Transport options are diverse, with domestic flights connecting major cities and safari destinations. Car rentals are available, but it's recommended to use 4x4 vehicles due to road conditions in more remote areas

Special Events and Festivals in 2025

In 2025, Kenya will host several notable festivals and events that showcase its vibrant cultural scene and diverse traditions. One of the most anticipated is the East African Art Festival in March, a three-day celebration of art, music, theater, literature, and crafts held in Nairobi. Another major event is the International Camel Derby and Festival in August, featuring camel racing, cycle races, and traditional entertainment in Maralal

For those interested in coastal celebrations, the Mombasa Carnival in November offers a colorful display of Kenyan culture with music, dance, and a grand street parade. Meanwhile, Jamhuri Day on December 12 commemorates Kenya's independence and republic status with parades, cultural performances, and fireworks

Additionally, the Beneath the Baobabs Festival in Kilifi offers a unique experience blending music, art, and sustainability and is recognized as Africa's first carbon-neutral festival

These events, alongside others like Eid al-Fitr and Christmas, promise an exciting year of celebrations across the country.

Future Developments in Kenya's Tourism Scene

As Kenya prepares for 2025, the country's tourism sector is set to evolve through a series of exciting developments and investments. The government's strategic plans, such as the "New Vision for Kenya's Tourism," aim to diversify the nation's tourism offerings beyond the traditional safari and beach experiences. This includes enhancing cultural and adventure tourism while tapping into emerging markets like India and China, a response to the growing demand for multi-faceted travel experiences

Alongside these efforts, Kenya's National Tourism Blueprint 2030 outlines long-term goals centered around marketing, infrastructure improvement, and attracting international investment

Tourism infrastructure is a key focus, with ongoing investments aimed at bolstering connectivity, especially in less-explored regions. This includes the development of regional tourism circuits that offer alternative experiences, such as the coastlines of the Indian Ocean and the country's lesser-known rural landscapes

In addition, Nairobi and Mombasa are enhancing their appeal with new hotels, restaurants, and luxury amenities tailored to international tourists. The government is also improving its security measures at tourist sites to ensure safety remains a priority

Looking forward, Kenya's tourism industry is also focusing on building a stronger global presence by increasing its online outreach and attending international exhibitions and road shows

With these strategies in place, Kenya's tourism sector is expected to rebound and grow in the coming years, potentially attracting more visitors and significantly boosting the local economy.

Conclusion

Kenya's tourism scene is poised for a vibrant future in 2025 as the country continues to build on its rich cultural, natural, and historical assets. With the introduction of new travel regulations like the Electronic Travel Authorization (ETA), easier access for international travelers is expected to further boost visitor numbers

The expanding infrastructure, including new hotels and attractions, alongside ongoing government support for tourism, positions Kenya as a competitive player in the global travel market

The diversification of tourism experiences—ranging from traditional safaris to cultural festivals and luxury retreats—will allow Kenya to attract a wider array of travelers. The rise in regional and international flights, as well as new developments in destinations like the Maasai Mara, Nairobi, and coastal towns, ensures that Kenya remains accessible while offering increasingly sophisticated options for tourists

Additionally, the government's efforts to enhance security and promote responsible tourism practices are key to ensuring a positive and sustainable growth trajectory for the sector

In conclusion, Kenya's tourism industry in 2025 is on track to achieve strong growth by capitalizing on its diverse offerings and improving visitor experiences. With strategic investments, global marketing, and a commitment to infrastructure and security, Kenya's appeal as a premier travel destination in Africa will continue to rise, drawing travelers from across the globe. As these developments unfold, Kenya's position as a global tourism hub will be solidified.

Printed in Great Britain
by Amazon